The Bond Effect

"How to do" the Bond Effect

Healthy Harvest
Cookbook
Companion to
Deadly Harvest

Nicole Bond
With
Geoff Bond

First edition © 2008 Nicole Bond
This publication is a creative work fully protected by all applicable rights.

COVER DESIGN: Jeannie Tudor
PRINTER: Printed and bound by CPI Antony Rowe, Eastbourne

ISBN-13: 978-0-9712852-6-2

General Website: www.TheBondEffect.com
General System Download site: www.SavvyEater.com
Special Cancer download site: www.BeatCancerNaturally.com

e-mail: admin@naturaleater.com

Natural Eating Company Ltd
55, Griva Digeni Street
Suite 73
8220 Chlorakas
Paphos
Cyprus

FOREWORD

Prepare yourself for a fine array of extraordinarily, delicious, colorful, and yes, believe it or not, *healthy meals*. They are only to be believed by experiencing them. The foods you will prepare from Nicole's cookbook collection will tantalize your taste buds and vitalize your senses into a new and exciting style of dining. Dining, of course, is what Nicole's foods are all about.

Dining incorporates all of the senses, activating not only the essential flavors of the foods, but the savory aromas for the nose, the pleasing placement and colors with romantic candle lighting for the eye, and the melodic musical melodies of vintage compositions that delight the ear. All are blended as one tasteful dish displayed before you on an artful palette designed to be enjoyed by your palate. All of this and more is to be experienced while taking the healthy diet to heart.

Dishes like Artist's Salad, Eggplant and Tahini Pie, Roasted Summer Vegetables, Curry Stir-fry Chicken Breast, Spicy Asian Fish and Chocolate Brownies, this is the ultimate in warm, earthy, healthful and natural eating — all created with a light touch.

This is the ultimate in warm, earthy, healthful and natural eating; all dishes are created with a light and sensitive touch, with your health and enjoyment in mind. It is a combination of international cuisines at its best.

Many of the recipes can be served as appetizers or as a main course. These recipes are perfect for occasions of all seasons. Winter, summer, spring, or fall, the meals will awaken a sense of newness and aliveness in your preparation, your presentation, and your appreciation for simple elegance. They are to be enjoyed and shared at the table in fellowship and friendship — these true treasures of life are exemplified by Nicole's healthy meals. Savor them.

Dr. James Melton
Visionary and Speaker

ACKNOWLEDGEMENTS

This work would not be complete without the ideas and experience of many followers and contributors. Conny Schober of Vancouver and author of It's Your Life! (a Bond Effect cookbook); Andy Irion, chef to Joe and Karalyn Schuchert at the Polo Ranch, Wyoming; Emma Moranval of Briançon, France; Hilary Harper of Cansiron Wood, England; Jeanne Bouvet of Annecy, France; Ingeborg Hoss of Provence, France; Jim and Dana Melton of The High Desert, California; and Peter Harris of Melbourne, Australia.

In addition, I owe a great debt to Rudy Shur, publisher of Geoff's book Deadly Harvest, for his invaluable advice in the setting out and presentation of cookbook recipes. If, in spite of his efforts there are any deficiencies or differences then these are my responsibility alone.

To these and all the other unmentioned contributors my grateful thanks.

HEALTHY HARVEST COOKBOOK
(Companion to Deadly Harvest)

CONTENTS

INTRODUCTION

Most of us try to do the right thing by our children and spouses, especially when it comes to feeding them. But we are confused by the conflicting messages. We are inundated with a plethora of diet books and cookery manuals claiming to show us the way to health and happiness. So what is so different about this one? The difference is fundamental. It is none other than feeding ourselves the way Mother Nature intended! That way we avoid stressing our bodies with foods it was never designed to handle. You will draw comfort from the knowledge that, by cooking our way, you are building the foundations for long, healthy lives.

We have designed all these recipes to conform to the principles of The Bond Effect. That is, they are in accordance with the basic guidelines formulated by nutritional anthropologist Geoff Bond. (See later). So when you follow these recipes you know that you are doing the right thing by yourself and your family.

This way of life does not need you to eat in an outlandish way. Your dinner guests will be surprised to find that they have been eating what seem like conventional dishes. Only you will know what subtle, yet vital changes in ingredients – and in cooking – you have made.

The principles behind the recipes of Healthy Harvest
Nature fashioned our bodies to be nourished in a particular kind of way – one that is special to us humans. However, for many generations, we have meddled in a state of ignorance with our food supply. The results have not always been happy ones, leading to "diseases of civilization" like cancer, heart disease, osteoporosis and diabetes.

Geoff's book Deadly Harvest (see back page) describes how this happened and how we finally know the right way to feed us humans – or as he puts it: "how to put the right gas in the tank". There are many surprises. We learn that many foodstuffs that we take for granted are secretly undermining our health. But the message is an optimistic one:

we do not need to be "food fascists" – we just need to *prioritize* what is important and what is not.

In this cookbook we focus on the important issues. Thus you will find that the emphasis is on removing bad carbs and bad fats and privilege the "good" ones. Consumption of fruits, salads and vegetables should be high. We aim to keep the intake of these up at around 75% of the diet and protein-rich foods down to 25%.

We strive to keep sodium (salt) low and potassium high. This happens quite naturally with the high intake of plant food but, in addition, we avoid processed food and keep added salt to a minimum. On the other hand, we obtain sumptuous flavors from the liberal use of aromatic herbs, fresh if possible.

We avoid "non-human" foods that give our bodies trouble with allergic substances (like gluten and lactose) and "antinutrients". (Antinutrients are naturally occurring poisons that plants make to fight off germs and funguses.)

All this might seem quite unusual, but in practice all we are doing is clearing out foods that have been making us sick for generations and replacing them with ones that work in harmony with our bodies. We invite anyone who is interested in knowing the background to these guidelines to check out Geoff's book, Deadly Harvest (see back page).

Goals

We want you to feel comfortable with this new way of eating. We have devised recipes that follow the guidelines, yet use readily available ingredients and are simple to prepare. As Geoff says, "we go hunting for our food in the same supermarket, we just hunt smarter!"

Nicole has tested each of the recipes many times to make sure they work well under all kinds of circumstances. We eat them regularly both for our family meals and when we are entertaining. They do not require huge expertise, just basic cooking skills and a willingness to try out new ways of preparing familiar dishes. Be prepared to be adventurous too! Try variations: experiment with different herbs and flavors!

What's in the Cookbook?

We set the scene for you in Chapter One. Here we help you with some of the basic equipment, ingredients and cooking techniques. Then, with Chapter Two we get into the recipes with simple sauces, dressings and dips. These, from Vinaigrette to Pearl Onion Relish, are always important to give great taste to salads, raw vegetables and other dishes. So often, conventional recipes are loaded with bad fats and bad carbs. But they don't have to be! Here we show you how.

Consumption of large quantities of plant food, preferably raw, is an important feature of the Bond Effect. That is where salads come in – we should all eat at least one good salad a day and Chapter Three focuses on those: from Artist's Salad to Moroccan Carrot Salad.

Chapter Four provides tasty recipes for soups of all kinds from the light Cold Tunisian Tomato Soup to a hearty Clam Chowder. In Chapter Five we come to main dishes. Some of them can be meals in themselves. We have divided the chapter into three classes of food: vegetable-based like Eggplant and Tahini Pie, animal based (poultry, game and meat) like Chicken Breast in Tomato and Onion or Hunter's Venison Stew, and seafood like Spicy Asian Fish.

Believe it or not, it is quite possible to devise wonderful desserts that conform to the Bond Effect. So, last but not least, with Chapter Six, we provide a range of remarkable sweetmeats from Chocolate Brownies to Rich Christmas Cake.

These dishes are for everyone! Whether or not you decide to live the Bond Effect way, you can be sure that dishes prepared from this cookbook will be the healthiest and tastiest that you can offer to your family and guests. Enjoy!

CHAPTER 1

INGREDIENTS and STAPLES:

1. Eggs:

We use eggs a great deal in our recipes. As such they are a "staple" ingredient in cooking the Bond Effect way. Contrary to common prejudice, eggs are a natural and healthy component of human nutrition. Fears about their cholesterol content are entirely misplaced: the body handles it in a healthy way. However, always choose eggs that are "omega 3 rich". They have a much better fatty acid profile: the omega-6 to omega-3 ratio is excellent. In addition, choose eggs from free-range hens that have been allowed to lead healthy, sanitary lives, free of antibiotics (often labeled 'organic').

Raw Eggs: In the last 20 years our food chain has become so polluted that raw battery hens' eggs are now considered a health hazard. The good news is that *organic* raw eggs are much safer. This is important in the case of *raw* eggs, which we use in just one recipe, Chocolate Mousse. Healthy people will have immune systems that cope well with the naturally occurring microorganisms present in eggs. However immune-compromised persons are nowadays obliged to avoid raw eggs.

2. Oils:

For cooking, we recommend that you use olive oil. It has better heat resistance than omega-3 rich oils like Canola. Always use oils frugally. Think about using an olive oil spray. Learn to sauté with very little oil. See "Stir-Fry and Sautéing" later. Avoid Canola oil which is sold as "heat resistant". That means that the good omega-3 has been stripped out of it.

For cold uses, such as salad dressing, use the omega-3 oils, for example Canola oil. To obtain the full benefit from Canola oil it needs to be cold pressed (you might need to look in a health food store for it). Other good oils are walnut (which must be made from raw walnuts) or flaxseed oil.

3. Vegetables:
Leave the peel on whenever practicable. Frozen vegetables are often fresher than the so-called fresh vegetables in the supermarket and make a perfectly acceptable alternative. The quality of fresh vegetables is more variable, so the cooking times can vary from those shown in the recipes. The weight of vegetables shown is gross, before cleaning and trimming. The portions of vegetables are larger than you are used to. It is always better to use *organic* fruit and vegetables if you can. But if you can't, don't let that stop you using regular ones.

4. Salads:
Don't forget that a salad can make an excellent meal in itself. (It is also a good standby when eating out.) Take plenty of mixed salad vegetables together with one of, say, salmon, sardine, tuna, mackerel, chicken breast, turkey breast, eggs, etc... It is all right to use canned fish.

Make your own salad dressings (for example recipe page 17) using one of the "good" omega-3 oils (see "oils" above).

5. Tomatoes:
To 'seed' tomatoes, cut them in quarters and carefully squeeze out the pips and juice.

6. Herbs and Spices:
Use fresh herbs wherever possible. Cut the leaves up with scissors as necessary.

For seed spices like pepper, cumin and coriander, the ideal is to use a mill for each and freshly grind them.

7. Dark, High Cocoa Mass Chocolate:
Some of the recipes call for chocolate. It must have a minimum of 70% cocoa solids. If you cannot find it then instead use:
4 oz bittersweet chocolate, minimum 50% cocoa solids, and
3 oz unsweetened baking chocolate, 100% cocoa solids.

8. Salt:

Many of the recipes suggest using salt "to taste". We urge you to keep this added salt to a minimum (the purist will not add any). You will find that, as you retrain your taste-buds, smaller amounts of salt have just the same powerful effect.

Instead of salt learn to use herbs to flavor your food. Lemon juice can give a similar taste sensation to salt. Garlic is good for this too. Mustard is great to give a kick to vinaigrette.

9. Almond (and other tree nut) Milk and Almond Cream (also called "Almond Butter"):

Note: in many countries, including the European Union, the terms "milk" and "cream" can only be used for dairy products "secreted by milk glands and obtained by milking". However, in the United States, there is no such restriction on these terms.

We use almond milk and almond cream in a number of recipes. It takes the place of cow (or soy) milk and cream, both of which we need to avoid. Almond milk and almond cream (or almond "butter") are commercially available but do read the labels carefully to avoid those brands that are loaded with added sugars.

Alternatively, you can make your own almond milk or cream. Either buy blanched almonds or blanche raw almonds to remove the skins. Then soak them overnight and pulp them, with the liquid, in a food processor. Add water to obtain the consistency desired.

You are not restricted to just almond products, most other tree nuts will do. Hazelnut or cashew milk and cream, for example are commonly available. (Often the cream is called "butter").

10. Almond Meal (or Almond "Powder", or Almond "Flour"):

We use almond meal in a number of recipes to replace wheat flour. As such almond meal is a "staple" ingredient for eating the Bond Effect way.

2. Receptacles:

Because you are now preparing large volumes of plant foods, scale up your ideas of receptacle size. Procure really large salad bowls, mixing bowls, woks and pans.

COOKING TECHNIQUES

Stir-fry or Sautéing:

Stir-fry is a frequently used 'healthy' cooking method. It may come as a surprise to know that traditional Asian stir-fry doesn't use oil at all. Chinese cooking just uses a couple of teaspoons of water. This is the ideal for us too but it is fine to use a tablespoon (or less) of olive oil. We give quantities in the recipes.

Oil and Water Stir-fry method:

Try this quick (5 minute) method of cooking vegetables. It starts by steaming and finishes by sautéing. Many vegetables soak up oil and this method greatly reduces the quantity of oil absorbed. Put ¼ inch of water into a large saucepan. Add the vegetables. (If they are frozen they might not need any water at all.) If you like, add a clove of sliced garlic and a bay leaf or a pinch of oregano. Add a teaspoon or two of olive oil according to the volume of vegetables. Cover tightly and cook on a high heat. Stir frequently. The vegetables cook fast, partly by boiling and partly by steaming. After three or four minutes, remove the cover and "stir-fry" continuously with a wooden spoon or spatula until all the liquid has evaporated. Continue until the vegetables are tastily browned on the outside. Do not overcook – this is a quick process – all done in 5 minutes. The vegetables should still be crunchy and be a beautiful golden brown. Always use plenty of herbs.

This is a healthy way of cooking: the vegetables are done quickly and gently in their own steam.

Oil and Water Roasting Method:

This is a sister method for *roasting*. It is much less aggressive than normal roasting, yet gives a delicious roast-like look and flavor.

Prepare the vegetables for roasting and put them in a roasting pan. Lightly coat them with olive oil and put them in the middle of the preheated oven. Now for the new part. Take a baking tray, half fill it with water (about $\frac{1}{4}$ inch), and place it in the bottom of the oven. Cook at the normal temperature for that dish (around 400°F, 200°C). What happens is this: the water in the tray starts to boil and make steam. The dish is partly steamed and partly roasted. It cooks in about half the normal roasting time and the vegetables come out a lovely golden color.

The high oven temperature boils the water which in turn keeps the cooking temperature at the water's boiling point (212°F, 100°C). In this way the vegetables are cooked more gently. They are also cooked more quickly in the *steam*. For these two reasons they retain more of their nutrients. Finally the high radiant heat browns the surface of the vegetables.

Sautéing Onions:
Many recipes call for onions to be gently cooked but not browned. This is the way to do it: Heat 1 tablespoon of oil in a non-stick saucepan (or use olive oil spray). Sauté the onion briefly on medium-high heat. When they start to stick, add some water and cook covered, on low heat. Once in a while, as they dry out, add a little water, to allow the onion to get a very soft consistency. But don't let them brown.

If you have frozen onion, the excess liquid needs to be driven off. Sauté, without oil, until the juices have evaporated. Then add the oil and proceed as mentioned above. Frozen onion cooks much faster.

Sautéing Mushrooms:
Place the sliced mushrooms in a frying pan without any oil or water. Put on a high heat and stir-fry continuously for a few minutes until they suddenly soften and release their juices. Reduce the heat and add a little olive oil. Optionally, add a little crushed garlic, lemon juice, and chopped parsley.

CHAPTER 2
Sauces, Dressings and Dips

Basic Vinaigrette
Yield: about 2 cups

This is a simple, light and salt-free vinaigrette for everyday use in your salads. The use of mustard and lemon juice means that we can dispense with salt. This recipe makes plenty for several uses. It is always easier to knock up a delicious salad when the dressing is ready to hand.

1 cup Canola oil
$\frac{1}{2}$ cup freshly squeezed lemon juice
$2\frac{1}{2}$ tablespoons Dijon mustard
$\frac{1}{2}$ teaspoon freshly ground black pepper
4 large cloves garlic, crushed
optional: add a variety of chopped fresh herbs, e.g. chives, parsley, basil, cilantro etc.

1. Place all the ingredients in a medium-size mixing bowl and, with an electric hand-mixer, blend until creamy, scraping down the sides of the bowl as necessary.
2. Keep refrigerated after use.

Artichoke Puree
Yield: 2 servings (as a side dish)

Can be served as a side dish, accompanying fish.
Can also be used as a raw vegetable dip.

1 can artichoke hearts (14 ounces)
3 large cloves garlic, roughly chopped
1 tablespoon canned capers, drained
3 tablespoons olive oil
2 tablespoons tomato juice, low sodium
1 tablespoon lemon juice
$\frac{1}{2}$ teaspoon grated lemon peel
2 tablespoons chopped fresh basil
salt to taste
freshly ground black pepper to taste

1. Combine all the ingredients in a food processor and blend coarsely.
2. Can be served hot as a side dish or chilled as a dip.

Basil Pesto
Yield: about ½ cup

This is a sauce that is frequently used to flavor soups in Provence and Tuscany. This sauce is also good as a dip for raw vegetables. Experiment with different amounts of the pine nuts and vegetable juice (or broth), to obtain the consistency desired.

2 tablespoons raw pine nuts
2 large cloves garlic, roughly chopped
1 cup firmly packed, trimmed fresh basil leaves (about 1 ounce)
2 tablespoons olive oil
4 tablespoons vegetable juice (from a can or carton)
½ teaspoon grated Parmesan cheese (the purist will leave it out)
salt (moderate) to taste

1. Place the nuts in a food processor or blender and grind into flour.
2. Add the remaining ingredients and puree until you obtain a very creamy texture.
3. Adjust the seasoning.
4. Keep refrigerated after use.

Black Olive Tapenade
Yield: about 2 cups

This is a traditional sauce from Provence, in the South of France. It is served as a spread on bread, but can also be served as a raw vegetable dip. If you want to use the tapenade as a sauce, then thin it down, by adding liquid from the olives.

2 cans black pitted olives (6 ounces drained weight each)
5 large cloves garlic, roughly chopped
2 tablespoons capers
4 tablespoons olive oil
2 teaspoons red wine vinegar or balsamic vinegar
2 teaspoons lemon juice
2 teaspoons thyme, fresh or dried
$\frac{1}{4}$ teaspoon freshly ground black pepper
6 tablespoons liquid, drained from the olives

1. Drain the olives and set aside the liquid (for thinning the sauce, if needed).
2. Place all the ingredients in your food processor or blender, and purée until a creamy consistency is obtained. No added salt is necessary, because of the already salty olives.
3. After use, refrigerate any leftovers.

Green Olive Tapenade
Yield: about 2 cups

This is a traditional sauce from Provence, in the South of France. It is served as a spread on bread, but can also be served as a raw vegetable dip. If you want to use the tapenade as a sauce, then thin it down, by adding liquid from the olives.

2 cans pitted green olives, (6 ounces drained weight each)
5 large gloves garlic, roughly chopped
4 anchovy fillets (canned in olive oil), roughly chopped
2 tablespoons capers
1 tablespoon Brandy
3 tablespoons olive oil
1 teaspoon Italian seasoning
6 tablespoons liquid, drained from the olives
optional: 1 pinch fresh-ground coriander

1. Drain the olives and set aside the liquid (for thinning the sauce, if needed).
2. Place all the ingredients in your food processor or blender, and purée until a creamy consistency is obtained. No added salt is necessary, because of the already salty olives and anchovies.
3. After use, refrigerate any leftovers.

Guacamole
Yield: 1½ -2 cups
(depending on the size of the avocados)

A classic recipe for this excellent dip – and it tastes better than anything you can buy in the shops!

2 ripe avocados
½ cup chopped tomatoes
2 tablespoons fresh lime (or lemon) juice
3 tablespoons finely chopped fresh cilantro
1 tablespoon finely chopped green onion
1 large clove garlic, crushed
1 teaspoon ground cumin
¼ teaspoon cayenne pepper
¼ teaspoon salt

1. Put all the ingredients in a medium-size bowl and mash with a fork or a potato masher.
2. Alternatively, blend all the ingredients (except the tomatoes) in a blender for 20 seconds. Add the tomatoes and blend for another 5 seconds.
3. Serve chilled.
4. After use, refrigerate any leftovers.

Nacho Cheeze Sauce
Yield: about 1½ cup

This sauce has a cheese-like flavor and is a recipe that will also appeal to vegans.

½ cup pine nuts (about 2 ounces)
½ cup sesame seeds (about 3 ounces)
1 large clove garlic, crushed
1 red bell pepper, seeded and roughly chopped
1 tablespoon fresh lemon juice
1½ tablespoon nutritional yeast flakes
¼ teaspoon salt, or to taste
freshly ground black pepper, to taste
4 drops Tabasco sauce, or to taste

1. Soak the nuts and seeds overnight (or at least for 3 hours) in water.
2. Rinse nuts and seeds in a sieve (not a colander).
3. Put all the ingredients in your blender or food processor and purée until you obtain a smooth consistency.
4. Chill and serve.
5. Refrigerate any leftovers.

Onion Curry Sauce
Yield: about 2 cups

Sauces don't have to be diet-busters! This is a delicious and safe to eat sauce, to give added depth and flavor to most vegetable and fish dishes.

1 tablespoon olive oil
1 medium brown onion (about 5 ounces), thinly sliced
1 teaspoon curry powder, or to taste
$1\frac{1}{2}$ cups vegetable broth or vegetable juice

1. Heat the oil in a non-stick saucepan and sauté the onion briefly on medium-high heat.
2. Mix in the curry. When the onion start to stick to the bottom of the saucepan, add $\frac{1}{4}$ cup vegetable broth and cook covered, on low heat, until the onions are soft and translucent, adding more of the vegetable broth if needed.
3. Add the remaining vegetable broth. The sauce is ready to serve.

Pearl Onion Relish
Yield: about 3 1/3 cups

Onions are a wonderful, nourishing supervegetable. This is an interesting way of preparing them with a sweet taste.
This dish is great as a kind of relish to serve with other vegetable dishes or with concentrated foods, such as the olive cake (see page 36). Unlike conventional relishes, this dish can be eaten freely. The small amount of raisins gives taste and some sweetness without increasing blood sugar surges significantly.

olive oil spray
2 packets (10 ounces each) frozen pearl onions
4 tablespoons raisins (about 2 ounces)
1 tablespoon coriander seeds
4 tablespoons white wine
1 tablespoon tomato paste
2 tablespoons balsamic vinegar
2 tablespoons olive oil
1 tablespoon fructose
$\frac{1}{2}$ teaspoon turmeric
freshly ground black pepper, to taste

1. Spray a large frying pan with the olive oil and spread out the frozen onions in a single layer. Sprinkle with the raisins and coriander seeds and start heating the onion on medium heat.
2. In the meantime place all the remaining ingredients in a small mixing bowl, and with a hand whisk, blend all the ingredients until smooth. Pour the mixture over the onions. Bring slowly to a boil.
3. Simmer covered for approximately 40-60 minutes, or until the onions are cooked, but still slightly crunchy.

Greek Almond-Garlic Dip (Skordalia)
Yield: about 1¼ cup

A classic Greek sauce which can be served as a dip, or served with chicken or fish dishes. As a variant use cold pressed, organic Canola oil instead of olive oil.

¾ cup blanched almonds (about 4 ounces)
4 large cloves garlic, roughly chopped
1 tablespoon lemon juice
1 tablespoon nutritional yeast flakes
½ cup extra virgin olive oil
½ cup hot water (more or less, if desired)
salt to taste
freshly ground black pepper, to taste

1. Place the almonds in a food processor or blender, and grind into flour.
2. Add the garlic, lemon juice and yeast flakes and purée until smooth.
3. Keep the processor running whilst you very slowly pour in the oil.
4. Blend in the water gradually to give the consistency you prefer.
5. Salt and pepper to taste.
6. Chill in the refrigerator before serving.

Tomato Sauce Provençale
Yield: about 1¼ cup

This highly flavored tomato sauce makes a fine condiment complement to such dishes, as broccoli loaf.....

1 pound ripe tomatoes
1 tablespoon olive oil
1 medium onion (about 4 ounces), finely chopped
3 medium cloves garlic, crushed
1 teaspoon dried Herbs of Provence (or Italian seasoning)
2 bay leaves
salt to taste
freshly ground black pepper, to taste
2 tablespoons chopped fresh parsley

1. In a medium-size bowl pour boiling water over the tomatoes. Set aside for 1 minute. Drain the tomatoes, peel off the skin, cut in quarters, seed and chop them. Set aside.
2. Heat the oil in a medium-size frying pan and sauté the onion until it is soft and translucent. Add in the garlic and sauté for 2 minutes.
3. Add the tomatoes, the Herbs of Provence (or Italian seasoning), the bay leaves and salt and pepper to taste.
4. Cook uncovered over medium heat. When most of the liquid has evaporated, reduce the heat. Simmer, uncovered, stirring frequently, until the tomatoes start to stick to the pan (this whole cooking process will take up to 30 minutes). Mix in the parsley.
5. Can be served hot or cold.

CHAPTER 3
Salads and Starters

Artist's Salad
Yield: 4 servings

This exotic salad, redolent of the Levant, is a favorite recipe of Doros Theodorou, Manager of 5-Star Hotels in Mediterranean resorts. It uses the salad leaf arugula (also called rocket) which has a special strong and slightly bitter flavor.

2 cups roughly chopped fresh arugula (rocket) leaves
2 cups roughly chopped fresh cilantro leaves
3 cups thinly sliced mushrooms (about 6 ounces)
8 tablespoons vinaigrette (see recipe page 17), to taste
2 cherry tomatoes, cut in half

1. Put the arugula (rocket), cilantro and mushrooms in a medium-size salad bowl. Add the vinaigrette and toss well.
2. Serve on individual plates and garnish the center with one half of the cherry tomatoes.

Avocado Salad
Yield: 2 servings

This is a highly nutritious, satisfying salad. Don't hesitate to use it as a main course if you desire.

Vinaigrette:
4 tablespoons Canola oil
2 tablespoons freshly squeezed lemon juice
salt to taste
freshly ground black pepper, to taste
Staples:
2 cups thinly sliced brown or white mushrooms (about 4 ounces)
2 green onions, thinly sliced
3 cups fresh baby spinach leaves (about 2 ounces)
2 avocados, peeled, roughly cut into chunks
8 cherry tomatoes, cut in half

1. Take a medium-size salad bowl and blend with a hand-whisk all the vinaigrette ingredients together.
2. Mix in the mushrooms and the green onions. Add the spinach leaves and toss. Gently mix in the avocado chunks.
3. Decorate with the cherry tomatoes.

Bell Pepper Provençale
Yield: 4 servings

To make the dish more colorful, instead of 4 red bell peppers, you can use 3 red and 1 yellow or orange bell pepper (green bell peppers are less tasty).

4 medium red bell peppers
4 large cloves garlic, crushed
4 tablespoons olive oil
salt (moderate)
freshly ground black pepper, to taste
1 tablespoon chopped fresh basil leaves

1. Wash the bell peppers. Bake in a preheated oven at 400°F (200°C) for approximately 30-35 minutes, turning them once. Their skin should be wrinkled. Place the bell peppers in a plastic bag and close tightly. Let them cool off in the bag (alternatively: holding the bell pepper in tongs, sear it over a flame until the skin blisters, loosens and chars slightly).
2. Their skin can now easily be removed. Cut in half, to take off the seeds. Remove the stalks and ribs. Cut in strips of 1-inch.
3. Lay out the bell peppers in a serving dish.
4. Take a small bowl and, with a fork, mix together garlic, oil, salt, pepper and half of the basil. Pour this mixture equally over the bell peppers.
5. Keep the dish in the fridge until 15 minutes prior to serving. Best made 2- 3 hours in advance, or even the day before.
6. Prior to serving, sprinkle the remaining basil over the bell peppers.

Eggplant Sandwich Raphael
Yield: 4 servings

Delight your friends at a dinner party. These multicolored, multilayered "sandwiches" make a dish that is both spectacular and amazingly tasty, but also easy to make. [Note: this dish, with its cheese, is not for the purist]

2 very large eggplants (about 2 pounds)
1 pound large tomatoes
$\frac{1}{2}$ pound Mozzarella cheese
olive oil spray
1 cup fresh basil leaves (about 15 leaves per sandwich, garnish included)
4 tablespoons balsamic vinegar

1. Cut the washed, but unpeeled eggplants, into $\frac{1}{2}$-inch thick slices (you need to obtain 12 slices.). Set aside.
2. Cut the washed, but unpeeled tomatoes, also into $\frac{1}{2}$-inch thick slices. Set aside.
3. Cut the Mozzarella cheese into 8 slices. Set aside
4. Spray a baking sheet with the olive oil and lay out the eggplant slices.
5. Preheat the grill in your oven and grill the eggplant for about 7-8 minutes on each side, or until the eggplant is soft.
6. Spray a large baking dish with the olive oil. Place 4 single eggplant slices on the bottom of the dish.
7. Cover with the Mozzarella cheese.
8. Cover the cheese entirely with the tomato slices.
9. Place basil leaves over the top of the tomatoes.
10. Now place another eggplant slice on top, followed again by another cheese, tomato and basil layer.
11. Cover with one last eggplant slice.
12. Bake in a preheated oven at 360°F (180°C) for approximately 2 minutes, until the cheese is melting.
Place each eggplant sandwich on a small serving plate and pour 1 tablespoon of balsamic vinegar over the dish. Garnish with a few basil leaves.

Herby Mushrooms
Yield: 6 servings

This is Hilary Harper's interesting and creative Portabella recipe. Hilary, who lives in Kent, England, has been cooking the Natural Eating way for many years. Experiment with the coriander and vinegar quantities to suit your taste.

6 Portabella mushrooms, medium-size
olive oil spray
2 tablespoons olive oil
3 tablespoons raspberry vinegar (could be replaced by balsamic vinegar)
1 tablespoon chopped fresh cilantro
3 medium cloves garlic, crushed
3 cherry tomatoes, cut in half
3 cups mixed green leaves (about 3 ounces), e.g. watercress, arugula (rocket), baby spinach, trimmed and washed

1. Wipe the mushrooms carefully with a paper kitchen towel. Trim the end of the stems.
2. Spray the bottom of a medium-size baking dish lightly with olive oil. Place the mushrooms, stalk-side up, in the baking dish.
3. Whisk with a fork in a small mixing bowl the olive oil, the vinegar, the cilantro and the garlic. Divide among the upturned mushrooms. Cap each mushroom stem with a tomato half.
4. Cover with aluminum foil and cook at 320°F (160°C) for approximately 25 minutes, or until done (in a microwave it takes only approximately 10 minutes at 600 watts power).
5. Serve the mushrooms on a bed of green leaves. Can be eaten warm or cold.

Mango Starter
Yield: 2 servings

The mango starter is naturally sweet and slightly glycemic. In these small quantities it is nevertheless acceptable.

1 mango (about 1 pound)
1 tablespoon olive oil
3 tablespoons mango sauce (see recipe below)
1 tablespoon chopped fresh mint leaves (or lemon balm leaves)
freshly ground black pepper, to taste

1. Peel the mango and carve the flesh around the stone into slices. Divide and lay out between 2 plates.
2. Drizzle with olive oil and mango sauce (see recipe below).
3. Sprinkle with the mint leaves and pepper to taste.

Mango Sauce: Yield about $1\frac{1}{4}$ cup
1 mango (about 1 pound)
2 tablespoons raspberry vinegar, or to taste (can be replaced by another fruit vinegar or white wine vinegar)

Peel the mango. Carve the flesh around the stone and in a blender puree the flesh with the vinegar to obtain the consistency you desire. Pour into a bottle and keep in the fridge.

Moroccan Carrot Salad
Yield: 6 servings

The quantities of herbs are quite high and they are rich in wondrous micronutrients. Experiment with different quantities of herbs to suit your taste. Fresh parsley and mint are best, but if not, then use dried ones. You need only a quarter of the fresh volume. In contrast, fresh garlic is more potent than ready-to-use preparations.

This salad tastes best when prepared an hour ahead of time and set out at room temperature to develop full flavor. It keeps up to 5 days in the refrigerator.

$1\frac{1}{2}$ pound carrots, peeled

2 cups chopped fresh parsley

1 cup chopped fresh mint

Vinaigrette:

5 tablespoons Canola oil, organic, first pressing

4 tablespoons lemon juice, preferably freshly squeezed

1 teaspoon (or to taste) ground cumin

salt (moderate) to taste

freshly ground black pepper, to taste

1 dash Tabasco Sauce (optional)

6 large cloves garlic, crushed

1. Grate (or slice) the carrots in a food processor. Set aside

2. In a large salad bowl make the vinaigrette, by mixing all the ingredients together with a hand-whisk.

3. Add the carrots, parsley and mint and toss well.

4. Cover the salad until it is ready to serve.

Salads and Starters

Olive Cake
Yield: 12 servings (slices)

This makes a concentrated, high protein dish, suitable to serve as an appetizer or as an accompaniment to a main meal.

1 can pitted black olives (6 ounces, drained weight)
5 eggs
1 pinch of nutmeg
$\frac{1}{2}$ teaspoon garlic powder
10 drops Tabasco sauce
3 tablespoons olive oil
2 tablespoons white wine
about $1\frac{1}{2}$ cups almond meal (about 5 ounces - more or less, depending on the size of the eggs)
1/3 cup (about 1 ounce) grated Swiss cheese – the purist will leave it out
salt (moderate) to taste
freshly ground black pepper, to taste
olive oil spray

1. Rinse the olives in a colander. Drain and cut them in half.
2. Take a medium-size bowl and, with an electric hand-mixer, beat the eggs with the nutmeg, garlic powder and Tabasco sauce.
3. Mix in the oil, white wine, almond meal and blend all well together, to obtain a smooth consistency.
4. With a fork stir in the cheese and the olives. Salt and pepper to taste. Be frugal with the added salt. There is already a lot of salt in the olives (even rinsed) and the cheese. The mixture should have the consistency of a very thick soup.
5. Spray with olive oil a loaf mold (10-inches long, 5-inches wide, 3-inches high) and fill with the mixture.
6. Bake in a preheated oven at 360F (180°C) for 40-45 minutes. Check the center of the dish for complete doneness.

Red Bell Peppers with Tomato
Yield: 4 servings

A tasty and interesting way to prepare red bell peppers.

olive oil spray
4 large red bell peppers
4 medium tomatoes
8 canned anchovy fillets
2 large cloves garlic
freshly ground black pepper, to taste
about 40 fresh basil leaves

1. Cut the bell peppers in half, remove the seeds, but leave the stalks. Spray a roasting tray with olive oil and lay out the bell pepper halves, cut side up.
2. Put tomatoes in a bowl and pour boiling water over them. Leave them for one minute, then drain and slip the skins off. Cut the peeled tomatoes in quarters and place two quarters in each pepper half.
3. Snip one anchovy fillet per half-pepper into rough pieces and add to the tomatoes in each pepper half.
4. Peel the garlic cloves, slice them thinly and divide the slices equally between the tomatoes and anchovies. Season with the black pepper (the anchovies alone provide enough salt).
5. Spray olive oil over each pepper half.
6. Place the roasting tray on a high rack in an oven preheated to 360°F (180°C). Bake for about 40 minutes, or until the bell pepper is soft, but slightly crunchy.
7. Garnish with a few scattered basil leaves. Serve hot.

Tuna-Coleslaw Salad
Yield: 4 servings

An extraordinarily tasty combination of great, healthy ingredients – the tuna with its good omega-3 oils, the 'SuperVeg' (cabbage), the tomatoes, the garlic and onion - all full of great micronutrients. Your family will enjoy this so much that you might find that these quantities only stretch for 2 people.

Vinaigrette:
3 tablespoons Canola oil
3 tablespoons fresh lemon juice
3 tablespoons Canola Mayonnaise
3 large gloves garlic, crushed
3 green onions, sliced
freshly ground black pepper, to taste
salt to taste
Staples:
3 medium tomatoes (about 12 ounces), chopped
3 medium, pickled cucumbers (about 4 ounces), cut in small dices
2 can tuna in water ($4\frac{1}{2}$ ounces net weight each), drained
1 can black sliced olives (4 ounces drained weight), rinsed and drained
1 packet shredded white cabbage (coleslaw) - 16 ounces
(may be substituted by a whole cabbage, suitably shredded)
3 tablespoons chopped fresh parsley

1. Place all the ingredients for the vinaigrette in a small bowl and with an electric hand-mixer blend until smooth, scraping down the sides of the bowl as necessary.
2. Pour the vinaigrette in a very large salad bowl, mix in the tomatoes, pickled cucumbers, tuna and olives. Add the coleslaw. Salt and pepper to taste and toss well.
3. Prior to serving, mix in the parsley.

CHAPTER 4
Soups

Cold Tunisian Tomato Soup
Yield: 6-8 servings

A refreshing and tasty soup whose subtle flavors hint at the mysteries of Arabia.

4 pounds ripe Roma tomatoes, peeled and roughly cut
4 large cloves garlic, roughly chopped
2 tablespoons fresh lime juice
25 mint leaves, fresh
$\frac{3}{4}$ teaspoon salt (or to taste)
freshly ground black pepper, to taste
Garnish:
6 - 8 mint leaves
1 lime, thinly sliced

1. In a food processor or blender mix the tomatoes with all the ingredients, to obtain a smooth consistency.
2. Serve chilled in individual soup bowls.
3. Garnish with the remaining mint leaves and hook a thin lime slice on the rim of each cup.

Fennel Gazpacho
Yield: 6 servings

The interesting flavor of fennel brings a new excitement to this classic, thick, cold soup.

1 large fennel (about 10 ounces)
2-3 firm Roma tomatoes (about 8 ounces)
2½ pounds ripe tomatoes
1 tablespoon olive oil
1 medium onion (about 5 ounces), chopped
3 medium cloves garlic, crushed
1 teaspoon ground coriander
½ teaspoon freshly ground black pepper
1 teaspoon dried oregano
1 tablespoon balsamic vinegar
2 tablespoons tomato paste
salt to taste
2 cups vegetable broth or vegetable juice
1-2 tablespoons lemon or lime juice, to taste

1. Trim the green fronds from the fennel bulb and save for garnish. Cut fennel bulb into quarters. Chop 3 quarters roughly and set aside. Cut the remaining quarter into very small dices and set aside separately.
2. Cut the Roma tomatoes in halves, seed and cut in very small dices. Set aside.
3. Put the tomatoes in a large bowl and pour boiling water over them. Set aside for 1 minute. Drain the tomatoes, peel off the skin, cut in quarters, seed and chop them roughly. Set aside.
4. Heat the oil in a large non-stick saucepan and sauté the onion, until it is soft and translucent.
5. Add the garlic, coriander, pepper, oregano and sauté for about 2 minutes, until the spices give off their full aroma. Stir in the vinegar.

Soups

6. Add the roughly chopped tomatoes and tomato paste. Salt to taste.

7. Add the roughly chopped fennel quarters and the vegetable broth. Bring slowly to a boil. Simmer, uncovered, for approximately 20 minutes, or until the vegetables are cooked. Allow to cool.

8. Blend the mixture in a food-processor (or blender), to obtain a smooth consistency. Add the lemon juice to taste.

9. Add the fennel dices and Roma tomato dices to the soup.

10. Chill for several hours in the fridge. Prior to serving, chop the fennel fronds and sprinkle them as garnish over the dish.

New England Clam Chowder
Yield: 8 servings

This recipe was featured by the food editor Sue Rappaport, in the Southern California newspaper, the Desert Sun, in December 2002 (see it also on www.naturaleater.com).

Originally chowder was a hearty seafood soup, prepared in a "chaudière" (cauldron), by Breton fishermen in Newfoundland. The New England variant is made with clams, and it usually includes potatoes, flour and cream. The clams are a fine, conforming seafood, low in fat and cholesterol. We dispense with the three bad ingredients: potatoes, flour and cream and thicken with cauliflower puree. As an option, replace the almond milk by chopped tomatoes. This version is known as "Manhattan-style" chowder.

28-ounce can baby clams
1 tablespoon olive oil
5 green onions, thinly sliced
3 medium cloves garlic, crushed
2 pounds cauliflower purée (see recipe page 55)
2½ cups almond milk (less or more - as needed)
celery salt, to taste
freshly ground black pepper, to taste

1. Drain the clams in a colander, but collect the liquid, which will amount to approximately 2 cups (16 fluid oz). Set aside.
2. Heat the olive oil in a large saucepan and sauté the green onion and garlic briefly.
3. Add the liquid from the clams. Stir in the cauliflower puree and mix well. Add the almond milk to obtain the consistency you desire (add more or less almond milk). Bring slowly to a boil.
4. Add the clams and heat all through. Add the celery salt and pepper to taste (be frugal with the celery salt, because of the already very salty clam liquid).

Red Soup
Yield: 4 servings

A delicious soup that can be eaten cold or hot. It has a massive content of healthful tomatoes and bell peppers.

4 medium red bell peppers (about $1\frac{1}{2}$ pound)
28-ounce can chopped tomatoes,
(or 2 pounds fresh ripe Roma tomatoes, peeled, seeded and roughly cut)
3 tablespoons nutritional yeast flakes
2 teaspoons lime juice, or lemon juice
$\frac{1}{4}$ teaspoon salt
freshly ground black pepper, to taste
10 drops Tabasco sauce, or to taste
3 tablespoons chopped fresh basil (+ some leaves for decoration)

1. Wash the bell peppers. Bake in a preheated oven at 400°F (200°C) for about 30-35 minutes, turning them once. Their skin should be wrinkled. Place the bell peppers in a plastic bag and close tightly. Let them cool off in the bag.
2. Their skin can now easily be removed. Cut in half, remove the seeds, stalks and ribs and cut roughly.
3. Combine the bell peppers, the tomatoes and all the other ingredients in a food-processor or blender, and purée to obtain a smooth consistency.
4. Adjust the seasoning.
5. Serve, hot or cold, in individual bowls and decorate with the basil leaves.

Zucchini Soup
Yield: 4 servings

This is an attractive and interesting way to prepare that normally bland vegetable, zucchini.

4 cups vegetable broth, or vegetable juice
about 2 pounds zucchini, unpeeled and roughly chopped
1 medium white onion (about 4 ounces), coarsely chopped
3 medium cloves garlic, sliced
2 tablespoons chopped fresh parsley
salt to taste
freshly ground black pepper, to taste
1 egg yolk

1. Combine in a large saucepan the zucchini, onion, garlic and 1 tablespoon of parsley in the vegetable broth. Bring to a boil and cook for about 15-20 minutes. Salt and pepper to taste.
2. Place the mixture in a food-processor or blender and mix until smooth.
3. Pour the mixture back in the saucepan and bring slowly to a boil again. Simmer for another 2 minutes. Remove from the heat.
4. Put the egg yolk in a small bowl and add 1-2 tablespoons of warm soup (not boiling) to the yolk, before stirring it back into the soup.
5. Serve in individual soup bowls and sprinkle the remaining parsley over the top.

CHAPTER 5
Main Dishes
Vegetable Dishes

Andalusian Vegetable Medley
Yield: 4 servings
Makes a great main dish or a tasty (cold) party snack.

1 tablespoon olive oil
2 medium red onion (about 10 ounces), sliced
2 red bell peppers (about 1 pound), seeded and cut into 1-inch strips
6 cloves elephant garlic, sliced
2 tablespoons balsamic vinegar
2 tablespoons soy sauce, low sodium
freshly ground black pepper, to taste
1 big eggplant (about 1 pound), unpeeled, cut into $\frac{1}{2}$-inch slices
salt (moderate)

1. Heat the oil in a big, non-stick frying pan (or wok) and sauté the onion, bell pepper and elephant garlic for about 10 minutes, stirring frequently.
2. Stir in the vinegar, 1 tablespoon of the soy sauce and sprinkle with pepper. Sauté all together for 2 minutes.
3. Add the eggplant slices and sprinkle with the remaining tablespoon of soy sauce. Add pepper to taste. Press the eggplant slices gently into the mixture. Cover, bring to a boil. Then reduce the heat and simmer gently, meanwhile folding the eggplant into the mixture. Simmer for about 30-40 minutes, or until the eggplant is done.
4. If there is too much liquid, cook uncovered for a few minutes, until the liquid has evaporated, or if the vegetables are already very soft, simply remove the excess liquid with a spoon. Salt to taste, but be very frugal, because of the already salty soy sauce.
5. Can be served hot or cold.

Bohemian Red Cabbage
(Rotkraut)
Yield: 4 servings

This delicious dish has its origins in Central Europe. Traditionally this dish is cooked for up to $1\frac{1}{2}$ hours, until the cabbage is really limp. However, nutritionally speaking, the less the cabbage is cooked, the better. Try cooking for no more than 30 minutes. Bohemian Red Cabbage is particularly well accompanied by a portion of game, such as venison or pheasant.

1 red cabbage (about 2 pounds), thinly shredded
1 tablespoons olive oil
1 medium red onion (about 5 ounces), thinly chopped
2 tablespoons caraway seeds
$\frac{1}{2}$ cup balsamic vinegar
1 tablespoon fructose
1 teaspoon allspice
1 green apple, unpeeled, grated
salt to taste
freshly ground black pepper, to taste

1. Steam the cabbage in your steamer for about 10 minutes. Drain and set aside.
2. Meanwhile heat the oil in a large saucepan and sauté the onion until soft and translucent, but not brown.
3. Add the caraway seeds and sauté briefly. Stir in the vinegar, fructose and allspice and sauté for 2 minutes.
4. Mix in the grated apple.
5. Add the cabbage. Season with salt and pepper to taste. Stir thoroughly, to coat the cabbage evenly with all the ingredients.
6. Cover and bring slowly to a boil. Simmer on very low heat for 20-30 minutes, stirring once in a while, to avoid the cabbage sticking to the pan.
7. Adjust the seasoning, if necessary and check for doneness. The cabbage should be very tender and soft.

Bok Choy with Mushrooms
Yield: 2 servings

A tasty and interesting way to prepare the super vegetable, bok choy.
This dish is prepared entirely in the microwave oven.

1 pound bok choy
2 cups oyster mushrooms (about 5 ounces)
$\frac{1}{2}$ teaspoon sesame oil
1 tablespoon light soy sauce
1 tablespoon oyster sauce
1 tablespoon sesame seeds

1. Coarsely shred the leaves of the bok choy. Cut the trimmed stems in half lengthways. Rinse under cold water. Place bok choy stems around the edge of a large shallow microwave-safe dish. Place leaves in the center. No need to add water, as there is enough left from the rinsing process.
2. Cover and cook on High (about 600-650 watts) for about 5 minutes, stirring halfway through. Stems should be just tender.
3. Let stand for a while in a large colander to drain, until no liquid is left.
4. Cut large mushrooms in half and combine with the remaining ingredients in a large microwave-safe bowl or dish.
5. Cover and cook on High (about 600-650 watts) for about 3 minutes, or until done, stirring halfway through.
6. Mix in the drained bok choy and cook, covered, for about 1 minute, or until hot.

Broccoli Gratin
Yield: 4 servings

A fine combination of vegetation and protein, in a healthy ratio of 6 to 1.
The cheese is present only in condiment quantities (the purist will leave it out). This dish can be eaten on its own or served with a salad.

2 pounds broccoli florets, fresh or frozen
olive oil spray
4 medium tomatoes (a good pound)
2 large white onions (about 11 ounces), thinly sliced
salt to taste
freshly ground black pepper, to taste
4 eggs
2 tablespoons water
1 teaspoon thyme, fresh or dried
1 tablespoon grated Parmesan cheese (the purist will leave it out)

1. Cook the broccoli florets in slightly salted, boiling water for approximately 3 minutes. The broccoli should still be firm and crunchy. Drain in a colander.
2. Spray a large baking dish with the olive oil and lay out the broccoli florets on the bottom.
3. Meanwhile place the tomatoes in a bowl and pour boiling water over them. Set aside for one minute. Drain, slip the skins off and seed. Cut into $\frac{1}{2}$-inch squares. Set aside in a colander.
4. Spray a small non-stick frying pan with the olive oil and sauté the onion, until it is soft and translucent.
5. Lay out the onion amongst the broccoli florets in the baking dish. Place the tomato squares in between the other vegetables. Salt and pepper to taste.

Main Dishes – Vegetable Dishes

6. In a small bowl, with a hand whisk, beat the eggs and the water. Salt and pepper to taste. Mix in the thyme.
7. Pour the eggs evenly over the vegetables. Sprinkle the cheese over the top (the purist will leave it out).
8. Bake in a hot oven at 360° F (180° C) for approximately 30 minutes. Check for doneness.

Broccoli Loaf
Yield: 4 –6 servings

This dish is delicious served either hot or cold. The little bit of cheese is a slight lapse and the purist can leave it out.

olive oil spray
1 pound frozen broccoli florets
2 medium cloves garlic, crushed
4 tablespoons vegetable broth, or vegetable juice
salt to taste
freshly ground black pepper, to taste
3 eggs
1 tablespoon olive oil
1 pinch nutmeg powder
4-6 drops Tabasco, to taste
1 tablespoon grated Swiss cheese (the purist will leave it out)

1. Take two florets of broccoli and set aside for decoration.
2. Spray a medium-size frying pan with the olive oil and sauté the rest of the broccoli rapidly.
3. Add the garlic and vegetable broth (or juice). Salt and pepper to taste. Sauté for about 10 minutes. The broccoli should stay crunchy.
4. Spray a loaf mold (10-inches long, 5-inches wide, 3-inches high) and spread out the broccoli on the bottom.
5. In a medium-size mixing bowl, and with a hand-whisk, beat the eggs with the olive oil, nutmeg, Tabasco, salt and pepper to taste. Stir in the cheese with a fork.
6. Pour the mixture over the broccoli in the mold. Carefully press the broccoli down into the liquid to expel air and to keep it, as much as possible, under the surface of the liquid.
7. Bake in a hot oven at 340°F (170°C) for about 35 minutes. Check the eggs for doneness.

Brussels Sprouts Gratin
Yield: 4 servings (as a main dish)

An excellent way to make an unexpectedly tasty dish out of Brussels sprouts.

This is a complete meal in itself and ideal as a main dish. It is very healthful too, both cauliflower and Brussels sprouts being "super vegetables" and the eggs providing a good fatty acid balance.

2 packets frozen Brussels sprouts (1 pound each)
olive oil spray
4 eggs
2 pinches nutmeg
2 cups cauliflower puree (about 12 ounces), homemade (see recipe page 55)
6 tablespoons vegetable broth, or vegetable juice
2 large cloves garlic, crushed
2 tablespoons Parmesan cheese (the purist will leave it out)
salt to taste
freshly ground black pepper to taste
5-10 drops Tabasco sauce, or to taste

1. Defrost and cook the Brussels sprouts, following the instructions on the packet. Drain and chop roughly.
2. Spray a large baking dish with the olive oil and spread out the Brussels sprouts on the bottom.
3. Meanwhile beat the eggs with the nutmeg in your food-processor. Add the cauliflower puree, the vegetable broth, the garlic and 1 tablespoon of Parmesan cheese. Salt to taste sparingly. Add the pepper and Tabasco sauce to taste.
4. Pour the mixture equally over the Brussels sprouts. Sprinkle the remaining cheese over the top of the dish.
5. Bake in a preheated oven at 360°F (180°C) for about 20 minutes, or until the top of the dish is golden brown.

Carrots Sautéed in Cumin
Yield: 4 servings

This is a creative way of using flavors and herbs to add zest to the common-or-garden carrot. This is a salt-free dish.

2 pounds carrots, sliced
2 tablespoons olive oil
2 tablespoons cumin seeds
freshly ground black pepper, to taste
2 teaspoons lemon juice
3 tablespoons chopped fresh parsley

1. Heat a wok or large non-stick frying pan. Add the carrots and sauté on high heat for a few minutes, stirring all the time, until the carrots start to brown a bit. Turn down the heat.
2. On medium heat add the cumin seeds, the olive oil, pepper to taste. Toss well to coat the carrots and cook, stirring frequently for about 15-20 minutes (the cooking time is variable, depending on the quality of the carrots).
3. Mix in the lemon juice. Check for doneness.
4. Prior to serving, mix in the parsley and heat through.

Cauliflower Bake
Yield: 4 servings (as a main dish)

Cauliflower is one of the "super" vegetables and this recipe is a fine way to prepare this vegetable. It also includes lashings of onion and mushroom. Traditionally this dish is garnished with melted cheese (the purist will leave it out).

1 pound cauliflower florets, fresh or frozen
olive oil spray
salt to taste
freshly ground black pepper, to taste
1 big white onion (about 7 ounces), sliced
2 large cloves garlic, crushed
4 cups sliced mushrooms (about 8 ounces)
4 eggs
4 tablespoons vegetable broth, or vegetable juice
2 pinches ground nutmeg
optional (the purist will leave it out):
2 tablespoons grated Parmesan cheese,
or: 4 thin slices Swiss or Cheddar cheese

1. Steam or microwave the cauliflower florets, until still crunchy. Drain excess liquid.
2. Spray a large baking dish with the oil and spread out the florets. Salt and pepper to taste.
3. Meanwhile coat a medium-size nonstick frying pan with the olive oil and sauté the onion, until it is soft and translucent.
4. Add the garlic. Mix in the mushrooms, stirring constantly, until they release their juices. Salt and pepper to taste.
5. Add the mushroom mixture to the baking dish and arrange to fill in the spaces in between the cauliflower florets.
6. Take a medium-size mixing bowl and with a hand-whisk beat the eggs, together with the vegetable broth (or vegetable juice), the nutmeg and salt and pepper to taste.

7. Pour the egg mixture evenly over the top of the vegetables and in between the spaces.

8. Optional: sprinkle the Parmesan cheese over the top of the dish (traditionally this dish is garnished with melted cheese, but the health purist will leave it out).

9. Bake in a preheated oven at 360°F (180°C) for around 15-20 minutes (or until the top of the dish is golden brown). (If you choose the Swiss or Cheddar cheese version: garnish with the cheese when the dish is already cooked. Switch off the oven and return the dish to the still hot oven for approximately 2 minutes, or until the cheese is melted.)

Cauliflower Puree
(mock mashed potato)
Yield: 2 to 4 servings

Thanks to Andy Irion, Chef to the Polo Ranch, Bighorn, Wyoming, for this recipe and for the creative ways it can be used to replace flour and potato.

This is a puree that is intended to be eaten just as it is - it closely resembles mashed potato. Your unsuspecting guests will not be able to tell the difference! But of course it has all the advantages of the "supervegetable" - cauliflower - and none of the drawbacks of potato. It is also a wonderful, healthful product for thickening soups and sauces. You thus avoid the use of flour and other undesirable, bad carbohydrate thickeners.

1 pound cauliflower florets, fresh or frozen
1 small white onion (about 3 ounces), cut in quarters
2 tablespoons olive oil
$\frac{1}{2}$ teaspoon salt
freshly ground black pepper, to taste
2 pinches of nutmeg
only if needed: 1-2 tablespoons vegetable broth, or vegetable juice
optional: 1 can chopped black olives (4-ounce drained weight)

1. Steam the cauliflower florets, together with the onion, until tender.
2. Put the vegetables in a food processor (or blender), together with the oil, salt, pepper and nutmeg. Blend to obtain a smooth consistency. Depending on the quality of the cauliflower, you might need more liquid to obtain this result. Hence add a little vegetable broth (or juice) if needed.
3. Optional: If you want to serve the cauliflower puree as a side-dish (and not use it as a thickener), mix in the chopped olives.

Curried Cabbage
Yield: 4 servings

Enjoy this succulent dish – an unusual and tasty way of preparing a great combination of cabbage, tomato and onion.

1 tablespoon olive oil
1 big white onion (about 8 ounces), thinly sliced
4 large cloves garlic, crushed
1 teaspoon grated fresh ginger
$\frac{1}{2}$ green pepper, seeded and finely chopped
2 teaspoon hot curry powder
1 teaspoon mustard seeds
$1\frac{1}{2}$ - 2 pounds white cabbage, thinly shredded
4 Roma tomatoes (about 12 oz), unpeeled and roughly chopped
salt to taste
freshly ground black pepper, to taste

1. Heat the oil in a large saucepan and sauté the onion briefly, until soft and translucent, but not brown.
2. Add the garlic, ginger, green pepper, curry powder and the mustard seeds. Sauté on low heat for about 2 minutes.
3. Add the cabbage and sauté on medium-high heat for 3 minutes.
4. Mix in the tomatoes. Salt and pepper to taste and sauté briefly on high heat for another 2 minutes.
5. Reduce heat and simmer, covered, for about 10-15 minutes, or until the cabbage is cooked, but still crunchy.

'Quick-Fix' Variation (Yield: 2 servings)

1 tablespoon olive oil
1 cup (about 6 ounces) frozen chopped white onion
3 medium cloves garlic, crushed
1 teaspoon ground ginger
1 teaspoon hot curry powder
$\frac{1}{2}$ teaspoon mustard seeds
1 'Ready Pack' (12 ounces) Angel Hair Coleslaw
1 small can tomatoes (14 ounces), drained
salt and freshly ground black pepper, to taste

Main Dishes – Vegetable Dishes

Eggplant and Tahini Pie
Yield 6-8 servings

An interesting way to make an appetizing and unusual dish of eggplant.

2 big or 3-4 medium-size eggplants (about 2 pounds)
1 cup thick, ready-made tomato sauce (about 8 ounces)
1 tablespoon lemon juice
¾ cup (about 6 ounces) ready-made sesame paste ("tahini")
4 medium cloves garlic, crushed
2 tablespoons olive oil
2 tablespoons light soy sauce
Tabasco sauce, to taste
2 eggs
2 tablespoons chopped fresh basil
freshly ground black pepper, to taste
olive oil spray
Garnish:
8 cherry tomatoes, cut in half

1. Prick the eggplants all over with a fork and roast them in a hot oven at 400°F (200°C) for around 45 minutes, turning them once (the eggplant flesh should be soft in the middle). Set aside to cool down.
2. Peel the eggplants and place in a food processor. Add all the ingredients and blend to a smooth consistency.
3. Spray a baking-dish (ideally about 10-inches diameter) with the olive oil and fill with the mixture. Spray the top of the pie lightly with the olive oil.
4. Bake for 20 minutes in a hot oven at 360°F (180°C).
5. Take the dish out of the oven and decorate with the cherry tomato halves (cut-side upwards) and bake for another 20 minutes. Check for doneness.

Emma's Ratatouille
Yield: 4 servings

Ratatouille is a traditional vegetable dish from the South of France. This recipe was perfected by Emma Moranval, a Bond Effect adept, living in Briançon in the French Alps.
With the left-overs you can make a great vegetable omelet.

1 tablespoon olive oil
2 medium-big red onion (about 10 ounces), thinly sliced
4 large cloves garlic, crushed
3 tablespoons tomato paste
2 teaspoons Italian seasoning
$\frac{1}{2}$ teaspoon chili sauce, e.g. Sambal Oelek
1 pound fresh tomatoes, roughly chopped
1 pound eggplant, unpeeled and cut into 1-inch cubes
salt to taste
freshly ground black pepper, to taste
1 pound red bell peppers, seeded and cut in 1-inch strips
2 medium zucchini (about 12 ounces), unpeeled and cut into $\frac{1}{2}$-inch slices

1. Heat the oil in a large pot and sauté the onion, until soft and translucent, but not brown. Add the garlic and sauté shortly.
2. Mix in the tomato paste, the Italian seasoning and the chili sauce.
3. Add the tomatoes and sauté for about 10 minutes.
4. Mix in the eggplant and salt and pepper to taste. Sauté for another 10 minutes.
5. Add the peppers and zucchini to the pot. Salt and pepper to taste.
6. Simmer covered for about 25 minutes, or until all the vegetables are cooked.

Fennel Casablanca
Yield: 2 servings

All the exotic flavors of the mysterious east are in this recipe from Morocco.

2 medium fennel bulbs (about 1 pound)
1 tablespoon lemon juice
3 tablespoons raisins (about 1 ounce)
1 tablespoon olive oil
1 big red onion (about 8 ounces), thinly sliced
$\frac{1}{4}$ teaspoon freshly ground cumin
$\frac{1}{4}$ teaspoon freshly ground coriander
salt to taste
freshly ground black pepper, to taste
$\frac{1}{2}$ cup pine nuts, or slivered almonds (about 2 ounces)

1. Trim the green fronds from the fennel bulb and save for garnish. Clean the fennel bulbs, remove the stringy parts (as with celery). Cut each bulb in half, place the halves in a bowl, cover with water and add the lemon juice. Prior to cooking, drain the fennel in a colander, dry each piece with kitchen paper, then cut in thin slices.
2. Soak the raisins in hot water for 5 minutes. Drain and set aside.
3. Heat the oil in a medium-size frying pan and sauté the onion, until it is soft and translucent, but not brown.
4. Add the fennel slices to the onion and sauté on medium heat for about 5 minutes, stirring frequently. Season with the cumin, coriander, salt and pepper to taste. Cover and simmer for some minutes until done, but still crunchy (the cooking time is very variable, depending on the quality of the vegetable).
5. Mix in the raisins and pine nuts and sauté briefly all together.
6. Prior to serving, chop the fennel fronds and sprinkle them as garnish over the dish.

Fennel Sautéed in Cumin Seeds
Yield: 2 servings

Fennel is often thought of as just a flavoring for other dishes. Here you find that it makes a fine dish in its own right.

2 medium fennel bulbs (about 1 pound)
1 tablespoon fresh lemon juice
1 tablespoon olive oil
salt to taste
freshly ground black pepper, to taste
1 teaspoon cumin seeds
1 tablespoon lime juice

1. Trim the green fronds from the fennel bulb and save for garnish. Clean the fennel bulbs, remove the stalks and the stringy parts (as with celery). Cut each bulb in half. Cut each half in three. Place the fennel in a bowl. Cover with water. Add the lemon juice.
2. Prior to cooking, drain the fennel in a colander. Dry each fennel piece with kitchen paper.
3. Heat the oil in a medium-size frying pan and sauté the fennel rapidly on both sides, stirring frequently, for about 5 minutes.
4. Salt and pepper to taste. Mix in the cumin seeds. Cover and simmer for some minutes, or until the fennel is done, but still crunchy (the cooking time is very variable, depending on the quality of the vegetable).
5. Mix in the lime juice.
6. Prior to serving, chop the fennel fronds and sprinkle them as garnish over the dish.

French Beans with Tomato
Yield: 4 servings

This is a superb, tasty and fully conforming plant food dish. Consume as much as you fancy.

4 medium tomatoes (about $1\frac{1}{2}$ pounds)
olive oil spray
5 medium cloves garlic, crushed
$\frac{1}{2}$ cup vegetable broth, or vegetable juice
salt to taste
freshly ground black pepper, to taste
1 teaspoon dried rosemary
1 pound French beans, fresh or frozen (green beans will do as well)
1 tablespoon chopped fresh basil

1. Place the tomatoes in a medium-size bowl and pour boiling water over them. Set aside for 1 minute. Drain the tomatoes, peel off the skin, cut in quarters, seed and chop them roughly. Set aside.
2. Spray a large saucepan with the olive oil and sauté the tomatoes for about 3 minutes.
3. Stir in the garlic and sauté for another 2 minutes.
4. Add the vegetable broth. Salt and pepper to taste and add the rosemary.
5. Bring to a boil. Add the beans and cook covered until done (depends on the kind of beans), but still green and crunchy.
6. Drain excess liquid, if needed. Mix in the basil and serve.

Medallions of Eggplant and Tomato
Yield: 4 servings

Serve this hearty dish as the centerpiece of any meal.

2 large eggplants (about $1\frac{1}{2}$ pounds), unpeeled
3 large, ripe, juicy tomatoes (about $1\frac{1}{2}$ pounds)
olive oil spray
salt to taste
freshly ground black pepper, to taste
2-3 teaspoons Italian seasoning
4 large cloves garlic, crushed
2 tablespoons chopped fresh basil
2 tablespoons olive oil
optional: about 12 ounces low moisture, part skim, Mozarella cheese (the purist will leave it out)

1. Cut the unpeeled eggplant in approximately $\frac{1}{2}$-inch thick slices. You should obtain about 16-20 slices.
2. Cut the tomatoes in slices of same thickness as the eggplant (there should be at least the same number of tomato slices).
3. Spray a baking tray or large baking dish with the olive oil and lay out the eggplant slices on the bottom. Salt and pepper to taste.
4. Sprinkle half of the Italian seasoning over the top. Place tomato slices on top of the eggplant slices (they should be covered entirely by the tomatoes). Salt and pepper to taste. Distribute the garlic evenly over the tomatoes. Sprinkle the remaining Italian seasoning, the basil and finally the olive oil evenly over the tomatoes.
5. Bake in a hot oven at 400°F (200°C) for approximately 30 minutes, or until the eggplant is soft and done.
6. Optional (not for the purist): cut the Mozarella cheese into thin slices and place on top of the cooked eggplant and tomato medallions. Put the dish back in the oven for 3 minutes, or until the cheese is melted and golden brown.

Nicole's Pizza
Yield: 4 servings

This is a fully conforming dish containing a good balance of vegetation and proteins of various kinds. It is popular with the kids too!

Sauce: yield about $1\frac{1}{2}$ - 2 cups
olive oil spray
1 medium brown onion (about 4 ounces), chopped
2 medium cloves garlic, crushed
1 teaspoon Italian Seasoning
14-ounce can chopped tomatoes
salt to taste
freshly ground black pepper, to taste
2 tablespoons chopped fresh parsley
Dough:
1 egg
3 tablespoons olive oil
1/3 teaspoon garlic powder
$\frac{1}{4}$ teaspoon salt
1 cup almond meal (about $3\frac{1}{2}$ ounces)
Dressing:
$1\frac{1}{2}$ tablespoon Dijon mustard
optional:
2 small tomatoes (about 7 ounces), cut in $\frac{1}{4}$-inch slices
2 tablespoons grated Parmesan cheese (the purist will leave it out)

Sauce:
1. Spray a medium-size frying pan with the olive oil and sauté the onion until it is soft and translucent.
2. Stir in the garlic and the Italian seasoning. Add the tomatoes and salt and pepper to taste.

3. Simmer, uncovered, stirring frequently, until you obtain a tomato sauce of thick consistency (the cooking process will take about 20-25 minutes). Mix in the parsley. Set aside.

Dough:

4. Meanwhile, in a medium-size bowl, beat the egg, with an electric hand-mixer, together with the olive oil, garlic powder and salt. Add the almond meal and blend well, until you obtain a pastry of thick consistency.

5. Spray a round baking dish (9½-inches diameter) with the olive oil and, by patting with a small spatula, spread out the dough in a thin layer (just to cover the bottom of the dish), leaving a low rim around the edge. Prick the bottom of the dough with a fork. Bake in a preheated oven at 360°F (180°C) for 3 minutes.

Dressing:

6. Take the dish out of the oven and, with a small spatula, spread the mustard in a thin layer over the pastry. Distribute the tomato sauce evenly on top. Optional: lay out the tomato slices in a circle over the top of the pizza dish.

7. Bake for 15 minutes or until the crust is golden brown.

8. If you choose the version (optional) with the Parmesan cheese, you need to take the dish out of the oven after 10 minutes and sprinkle the Parmesan cheese over the top of the dish.

9. Bake for another 5 minutes or until the cheese is melted.

10. If you have chosen to add the tomato slices to the dish, you will need 5 more minutes of baking time.

Quick Roasted Veggies
Yield: 4 servings (as a side dish)

A magnificent, colorful and tasty vegetable dish that is quick to put together – and that all the family can enjoy. It is a quicker, simpler version of Roasted Summer Vegetables, next page (page 66).

olive oil spray
2 medium red onions (about 10 ounces), cut through the root into four quarters, and then each quarter into half
1 big eggplant (about 1 pound), peeled and cut into 1-inch cubes
2 red peppers (about 12 ounces), seeded, cut into 1-inch squares
4 large cloves garlic
2 teaspoons Italian seasoning
2 tablespoons olive oil
salt to taste
freshly ground black pepper, to taste

1. Spray a large baking dish with the olive oil and spread out the onion, eggplant and pepper randomly.
2. Cut the garlic cloves in slices and distribute equally amongst the vegetables.
3. Coat the vegetables equally with the Italian seasoning and the 2 tablespoons of olive oil. Salt and pepper to taste.
4. Bake in a preheated oven at 400°F (200°C) for 30 minutes, then cover with an aluminum foil and bake for another 10 minutes.
5. Check the vegetables for doneness.

Roasted Summer Vegetables
Yield: 4 to 6 servings

This is a hearty and varied vegetable dish. It is quite filling and can easily serve as a complete meal in itself. Note the baked garlic bulb. This is a little-known but delicious way of eating garlic. It is possible to bake garlic on its own as a side dish.

2 medium onions
2 medium red bell peppers
2 large heads of garlic
2 Japanese eggplants (small eggplants)
2 medium tomatoes
1 small squash
2 medium zucchini
8 button mushrooms
olive oil spray
2 teaspoon dried thyme
salt (moderate), to taste
freshly ground black pepper, to taste
$\frac{1}{4}$ cup olive oil
$\frac{1}{2}$ cup vegetable broth, or vegetable juice

1. Peel the onions. Quarter them through the root, leaving the root intact if you can. Pre-cook the onions, by microwaving them for 2 minutes at 600 watts power.
2. Halve and seed the peppers, removing the stalks and any white membrane. Cut each pepper into quarters.
3. With a sharp knife cut the cleaned, but unpeeled garlic bulbs in half through the equator.
4. Cut the unpeeled eggplants in half lengthwise.
5. Cut the unpeeled tomatoes in half through the equator.
6. Cut the unpeeled squash lengthwise into 8 slices.
7. Cut the unpeeled zucchini in half lengthwise.

8. Clean the mushrooms gently with a kitchen paper and cut off the ends of the stalks.

9. Spray a roasting pan (12 x 18 inches) with the olive oil and distribute the vegetables (cut-side up), so that their colors make an attractive presentation.

10. Sprinkle the thyme, salt and pepper over the top.

11. Mix the olive oil with the vegetable broth and pour over the vegetables.

12. Cover the dish with an aluminum foil and bake in a preheated oven at 400°F (200°C) for 30 minutes.

13. Take the dish out of the oven and uncover. Except for the garlic, turn the vegetables.

14. Bake for another 20-25 minutes. The vegetables should be tender and browning but not disintegrating. The garlic (still in its husk) should be golden and soft.

15. Check for doneness and adjust the seasoning if needed.

Spicy Eggplant Quick Fix
Yield: 4 servings

This dish is quite quickly knocked together using eggplant and ingredients commonly found in the kitchen.
It mellows and takes its full flavor the day after preparation. The use of hot condiment (curry) is not aggressive: the quantities are modest, just enough to give zing to the bland eggplant.

1 tablespoon olive oil
3 medium eggplants (about 28 ounces), unpeeled and cut into bite-size pieces
2 medium red onion (about 10 ounces), sliced
2 tablespoons red curry paste (Thai or similar mild)
14-ounce can chopped tomatoes
1 tablespoon soy sauce, low sodium
freshly ground black pepper, to taste
optional: 3 twigs fresh basil

1. Heat the oil in a big, non-stick frying pan (or wok) and sauté the eggplant for about 5 minutes, stirring frequently.
2. Add the onion and sauté for another 2 minutes.
3. Mix in the curry paste and well coat the vegetables with the paste.
4. Add the tomatoes with their juice and the soy sauce. Pepper to taste.
5. Bring slowly to a boil, then simmer covered for around 20 minutes, or until the eggplant is done.
6. Optional: prior to serving, garnish with the basil leaves.

Spinach Hash
Yield: 2 servings (as a main course)

This is a dish that is quickly knocked up. You might be surprised by the choice of peanuts, but the raw, unsalted ones are tolerable, if you are not allergic to them. The purist can substitute chopped almond instead.

olive oil spray
1 medium onion (about 4 ounces), chopped (or instead: frozen chopped onion)
2 large cloves garlic, crushed
1 teaspoon paprika
2 tablespoons tomato paste
1 pound tomatoes, seeded and chopped (or instead: canned chopped tomatoes, drained)
salt, to taste
freshly ground black pepper, to taste
1 pound chopped frozen spinach
1/3 cup chopped raw, unsalted peanuts (about $1\frac{1}{2}$ ounces)

1. Spray a large frying pan with the olive oil and gently sauté the onion, until soft and translucent, but not brown.
2. Stir in the garlic and sauté for 2 minutes. Mix in the paprika and tomato paste.
3. Add the tomatoes and salt and pepper to taste. Gently heat together, stirring and mixing, for about 15 minutes.
4. Meanwhile defrost the spinach, following the instructions on the packet. Drain and add to the tomatoes and gently heat through.
5. Adjust the seasoning, if necessary. Check for doneness.
6. Mix in the peanuts towards the end of the cooking time and heat through.

Stuffed Eggplant
Yield: 2 servings (or 4 as a side dish)

Here we transform bland eggplant into a highly flavored and attractive meal.

olive oil spray
1 medium onion (around 5 ounces), chopped
14-ounce can chopped tomatoes
2 large eggplants (about 2 pounds)
3 gloves garlic
4 twigs fresh parsley
nutmeg
1 teaspoon ground coriander
1 teaspoon ground cinnamon
1 teaspoon fructose
1 tablespoon almond meal
salt to taste
freshly ground black pepper, to taste
2 teaspoons grated Swiss cheese (the purist will leave it out)

1. Spray a frying pan with the olive oil and sauté the onion until soft and translucent.
2. Add the chopped tomatoes. Cook uncovered over medium heat. When most of the liquid has evaporated, reduce the heat. Simmer, uncovered, stirring frequently, until the tomatoes start to stick to the pan (this whole cooking process will take up to 30 minutes).
3. Meanwhile cut each eggplant in 2 halves. Scoop out the flesh, using a knife and a spoon, leaving a thin layer of flesh close to the skin. Set aside the eggplant flesh.
4. Pre-cook the eggplant halves for 20 minutes in a hot oven at 360°F (180°C) for around 20 minutes, or until the eggplant is done.

Main Dishes – Vegetable Dishes

5. Meanwhile cut the eggplant flesh roughly and mix in an electric blender, together with the coarsely cut garlic and parsley.

6. Add the mixture to the tomato sauce.

7. Season with the nutmeg, coriander, cinnamon and fructose.

8. Mix in the almond meal. Salt and pepper to taste.

9. Stuff the eggplant halves with the tomato and eggplant mixture and lay out in an oiled baking dish.

10. Bake in a hot oven at 360°F (180°C) for around 15 minutes.

11. Sprinkle the grated cheese over the eggplant halves and bake for another 10 minutes, or until the cheese is melted and golden brown.

Stuffed Portabella Bake
Yield: 2-3 servings

A surprisingly simple dish to knock together – and quick too. The end result is impressive. Food-wise this is a fine and nutritious dish.

olive oil spray
1 white onion (about 5 ounces), chopped
2 medium cloves garlic, crushed
14-ounce can chopped tomatoes
1 teaspoon Italian Seasoning
salt to taste
freshly ground black pepper, to taste
6 Portabella mushrooms (about 6 ounces)
10 ounces frozen chopped spinach
optional: 6 Mozzarella cheese slices (the purist will leave it out)

1. Spray a medium-size frying pan with the olive oil and sauté the onion, until soft and translucent, but not brown. Mix in the garlic.
2. Drain half of the juice from the tomatoes and add the tomatoes to the pan. Mix in the herbs and salt and pepper to taste.
3. Wipe the mushrooms carefully with a paper kitchen towel. Remove the stems and set aside the mushroom cups. Trim off the ends of the stems. Finely chop the stems and add to the tomato mixture. Simmer uncovered for about 10 minutes.
4. Meanwhile defrost the spinach following the instructions on the packet. Drain the excess liquid from the spinach and discard. Add the spinach to the pan, stirring well. Adjust the seasoning.
5. Spray a medium-size baking dish with the olive oil and pour half of the sauce into the dish.

6. Distribute mushrooms, open cup upwards, on the sauce in the dish. Lightly pepper the mushrooms.

7. Fill the mushroom cups with the rest of the sauce.

8. Cover with aluminum foil and bake in a hot oven at 360°F (180°C) for approximately 15 minutes. Check the mushrooms for doneness.

9. Optional: cover the mushrooms with the cheese slices and place the dish under the grill for 2–3 minutes, or until the cheese is melted and golden brown.

Vegetable Lasagna
Yield 4-6 servings

This makes a fine plant-food dish with the vegetables layered in a tasty marinara sauce. It is like a Lasagna, but without the unwanted pasta.

1½ pounds red bell peppers
salt (moderate), to taste
freshly ground black pepper, to taste
6 sun-dried tomatoes
olive oil spray
3 smallish medium red onion (about 12 ounces), sliced
¾ pound mushrooms (about 12 ounces), sliced
1 tablespoon olive oil
2 large cloves garlic, crushed
1 jar or can (about 20 ounces) ready-made marinara sauce
(choose a "safe" one - read the ingredients list)
1 pound eggplant, unpeeled, thinly sliced
3 teaspoons Italian seasoning
2 medium zucchini (about 12 ounces), unpeeled and sliced
5 tablespoons red wine
optional: 3 tablespoons Parmesan cheese, grated (the purist will leave it out)

1. Wash the bell peppers and bake in a preheated oven at 400°F (200°C) for about 35 minutes, turning them once. Their skin should be wrinkled. Place the bell peppers in a plastic bag and close tightly. Allow to cool. It is now easy to remove the skin of the bell peppers. Cut them open and remove the seeds, stalks and ribs. Cut into wide 3-inch strips. Salt and pepper to taste. Set aside.
2. Pour boiling water over the sun-dried tomatoes and soak for 5 minutes. Drain, cut in dices and set aside.

3. Spray a medium-size non-stick frying pan with the olive oil and sauté the onion, until it is soft and translucent, but not brown. Set aside.

4. Sauté the mushrooms in the same non-stick frying pan, hot, no oil, stirring constantly, until they release their juices. Continue until all the liquid has evaporated.

5. Mix in the tablespoon of oil and the garlic. Salt and pepper to taste. Set aside.

6. Spray a large baking dish (14 x 10 inches) with the olive oil and lay out 1/3 of the marinara sauce on the bottom.

7. Layer the eggplant on top. Salt and pepper to taste. Sprinkle with 1 teaspoon of the Italian seasoning. Layer the zucchini on top. Salt and pepper to taste. Sprinkle with another teaspoon of the Italian seasoning. Spread another 1/3 of the marinara sauce on top. Lay out the bell peppers, followed by a layer of mushrooms and a layer of onion.

8. Mix the sun-dried tomatoes into the remaining marinara sauce and spread on top of the vegetables. Sprinkle with the remaining Italian seasoning.

9. Pour the wine equally over the dish and sprinkle with the cheese (optional-the purist will leave it out).

10. Bake uncovered in a preheated oven at 360°F (180°C) for approximately 1 hour. Check for doneness.

Winter Cabbage Stew
Yield: 2-3 servings

This hearty, chunky stew suits any time of year and is particularly welcome on a chilly evening. A great way to spice up that fine vegetable, cabbage.

1 tablespoon olive oil
1 medium white onion (about 6 ounces), roughly chopped
2 medium celery stalks (about 4 ounces), sliced
3 sun-dried tomatoes, chopped
2 medium cloves garlic, crushed
2 tablespoons mild curry paste
14-ounce can chopped tomatoes
½ white cabbage (about 1 pound), chopped
1½ cups vegetable broth, or vegetable juice
salt to taste
freshly ground black pepper, to taste

1. In a large saucepan heat the olive oil and sauté the onion, until it is soft and translucent, but not brown.
2. Add the celery, sun-dried tomatoes and garlic and sauté for 5 minutes all together.
3. Mix in the curry paste and allow the flavors to develop for 2 minutes.
4. Mix in the chopped tomatoes.
5. Add the cabbage and coat well with all the ingredients in the saucepan. Sauté, uncovered for 5 minutes.
6. Add the vegetable broth (or juice). Season with salt and pepper to taste.
7. Cover and simmer for about another 10-15 minutes, until the cabbage is cooked, but still crunchy.

Zucchini Curry Quick Fix
Yield: 4 servings (as a side dish)

A curry is often a good way to spice up bland veggies (like zucchini). Here, by the judicious use of other eastern spices and condiments, we conjure up a dish redolent of the exotic orient. Since this is a quick fix, we focus on the use of several ready-prepared ingredients, but nothing stops you from substituting fresh.

This dish tastes its best the day after its preparation.

olive oil spray
1 cup frozen chopped onion (about 4 ounces)
2 teaspoons ready-made chopped garlic
1 teaspoon ready-made chopped ginger
2 - 3 teaspoons red curry paste (Thai or similar mild), to taste
$\frac{1}{2}$ cup coconut milk
2 teaspoons light soy sauce
2 pounds zucchini, unpeeled and cut into bite-size pieces
2 teaspoons lemon juice
freshly ground black pepper, to taste

1. Spray a large frying pan (or a wok) with the oil and sauté the onion, until it is soft and translucent.
2. Mix in the garlic and ginger. Sauté all together for 2 minutes.
3. Blend in the curry paste, the coconut milk and soy sauce.
4. Add the zucchini and coat the veggies with the sauce.
5. Cover and bring slowly to a boil. Simmer for approximately 30 minutes, or until the zucchini is done.
6. Season with the lemon juice and pepper to taste.

Zucchini Dug-Outs
Yield: 2 – 4 servings

It serves 2 people as a main dish or 4 people as a side dish. The dug-out zucchini look like rustic native canoes piled high with their delicious, colorful cargos. This dish can be served either hot or cold.

2 pounds zucchini, unpeeled, cut lengthwise in 2 halves
salt to taste
freshly ground black pepper, to taste
1 teaspoon dried Italian seasoning
olive oil spray
1 medium white onion (about 5 ounces), chopped
4 large cloves garlic, crushed
14-ounce can chopped tomatoes, drained
1 tablespoon tomato paste
2 pinches ground nutmeg
$\frac{1}{2}$ teaspoon fructose
4-6 drops (or to taste) Tabasco Sauce
2 tablespoons crushed pine nuts
1 tablespoon chopped fresh parsley
optional: 1 tablespoon grated Swiss cheese (the purist will leave it out)

1. Carefully scrape out the soft pulp of the zucchini halves with a small spoon, so they take on the form of a dug-out canoe.
2. Take half of the pulp and chop it very thinly. Set aside (dispose of the other half).
3. Lightly salt and pepper the zucchini halves, sprinkle with half of the Italian seasoning.
4. Spray a baking sheet with olive oil. Distribute the zucchini halves.
5. Bake in a preheated oven at 400°F (200°C) for 20 minutes.

6. Meanwhile coat a medium-size, nonstick frying pan with the oil and sauté the onion, until it is soft and translucent, but not brown.

7. Stir in the garlic and the chopped zucchini pulp. Sauté all together for about 10 minutes.

8. Add the drained tomatoes, tomato paste and the rest of the Italian seasoning. Stir in the nutmeg, fructose, Tabasco drops and salt and pepper.

9. Adjust the seasoning, if desired. Sauté shortly for 2 minutes all together.

10. Mix in the pine nuts.

11. Distribute the mixture equally in the hollowed-out zucchini halves. Place them on the baking sheet.

12. Optional: sprinkle with the Swiss cheese (the purist will leave it out).

13. Bake in a preheated oven at 400°F (200°C) for around 15-20 minutes. Check for doneness of the zucchinis.

14. Prior to serving sprinkle with the parsley.

Zucchini and Tomato Gratin
Yield: 4 servings (as a side dish)

This is a fine, high plant-food dish.

3 medium white onions (about 14 ounces)
olive oil spray
2-3 zucchini (about 14 ounces)
1¾ pound ripe tomatoes (28 ounces)
salt to taste
freshly ground black pepper, to taste
5 large cloves garlic, crushed
2 teaspoons dried thyme, or more to taste

1. Peel the onion and cut them into thin rings.
2. Spray a small frying pan with the olive oil and sauté the onion, until soft and translucent, but not brown.
3. Spray a large baking dish with the olive oil and spread out the onion.
4. Meanwhile cut the unpeeled zucchini into fine slices and set aside. Finely slice the tomatoes to the same thickness as the zucchini and set aside.
5. Place on top of the onion layer the tomato and zucchini slices in alternating straight rows, so as to obtain red and green alternating colors.
6. Sprinkle with salt (moderately) and pepper to taste. Sprinkle the garlic and thyme equally over the vegetables.
7. Spray olive oil equally over the vegetables.
8. Bake in a preheated oven at 450°F (225°C) for approximately 30 minutes, tamping the vegetables from time to time with the back of a serving spoon. The vegetables should be slightly caramelized.
9. This dish can be savored either hot or cold.

Zucchini with Sun-dried Tomatoes
Yield: 4 servings (as a side dish)

A tasty and nutritious way of preparing zucchini. With the left-overs you can also make a great vegetable omelet.

$\frac{1}{4}$ cup sun-dried tomatoes
olive oil spray
2 medium red onion (about 8 ounces), thinly sliced
4 large cloves garlic, crushed
2 teaspoons grated ginger
$\frac{1}{4}$ teaspoon chili sauce
$\frac{1}{4}$ teaspoon ground cumin
$\frac{1}{4}$ teaspoon ground coriander
2 pounds zucchini, unpeeled, thinly sliced
salt to taste
freshly ground black pepper, to taste
1 teaspoon lemon juice

1. Soak the sun-dried tomatoes in hot water for 5 minutes. Drain, but keep $\frac{1}{2}$ cup of the liquid and set aside. Cut the drained tomatoes in small pieces and set aside.
2. Spray a large saucepan with the olive oil and sauté the onions, until soft and translucent, but not brown.
3. Mix in the garlic and ginger and sauté all together.
4. Add the chili sauce, cumin, coriander and the sun-dried tomatoes with the $\frac{1}{2}$ cup of their liquid.
5. Add the zucchini and salt and pepper to taste. Sauté for about 30 minutes, or until the zucchini are done.
6. Season with the lemon juice.

CHAPTER 5
Main Dishes
Poultry, Game and Meat Dishes

Chicken Breast in Tomato and Onion
Yield: 2 servings

Serve with a light green salad as a starter, and the meal is well balanced. Try to use organic, free-range chicken.

olive oil spray
1 skinless chicken breast (8-9 ounces), cut in half
salt to taste
freshly ground black pepper, to taste
1 large red onion (about 8 ounces), coarsely sliced
4 large cloves garlic, sliced
2 teaspoons dried Italian seasoning
5 Roma tomatoes (about 1 pound), cut in halves
1 tablespoon chopped fresh parsley

1. Spray a large frying pan with the oil and sauté the chicken breast halves briefly on both sides, until golden brown. Salt and pepper to taste. Set aside on a plate and cover.
2. Spray some more oil in the pan and sauté the onion slices for about 5 minutes, stirring frequently and adding a little water, when they start to stick.
3. Stir in the garlic slices and 1 tsp. of the Italian seasoning. Sauté briefly.
4. Place the tomatoes, cut-side down, in the pan. Sauté for a few minutes, then turn the tomatoes over. Salt and pepper to taste and sprinkle the remaining Italian seasoning over the tomatoes. Sauté on medium heat for another few minutes. If the vegetables stick to the pan, add a little water and/or cover the pan.
5. Place the chicken breast halves in the middle of the vegetables, cover and simmer for about 5-10 minutes. Check the chicken breast for doneness.
6. Sprinkle the parsley over the dish prior to serving.

Chicken Goulash
Yield: 4 servings

Conny Schober, fine cook (author of It's Your Life! cookbook) and Bond Effect practitioner, supplies us with this delicious recipe for that traditional Hungarian, spicy and slightly piquant soup, Goulash.

olive oil spray
1 skinless chicken breast (8-9 ounces), cut into $\frac{1}{2}$-inch cubes
2 medium white onions (8-9 ounces), finely chopped
2 cups tomato sauce, e.g. Napoletana style
2 cups chicken broth or chicken stock
1 red bell pepper, seeded and chopped
1 teaspoon paprika powder, or to taste
salt to taste
freshly ground black pepper, to taste

1. Spray a small frying pan with olive oil and sauté the chicken for about 1 minute from both sides, until golden brown. Remove and transfer to a large cooking pot.
2. In the same frying pan sauté the onion, until soft and translucent for about 2-3 minutes. Transfer to the chicken-pot.
3. Add the tomato sauce, the broth and the bell peppers. Season with 1 teaspoon (or to taste) paprika powder, salt and pepper to taste.
4. Simmer over medium heat for about half an hour or until the chicken is tender.

Main Dishes – Poultry, Game and Meat

Chicken Pot-au-Feu
Yield: 4 servings

A hearty and complete meal in itself. Rich in both vegetables and some chicken, this can be eaten to satiety.

olive oil spray
1 medium white onion (about 6 ounces), sliced
3 large cloves garlic, thinly sliced
2 teaspoons stir-fry spices
28-ounce can chopped tomatoes
1 cup vegetable broth, or vegetable juice
2 tablespoons tomato paste
$\frac{1}{2}$ teaspoon chili sauce
salt to taste
freshly ground black pepper, to taste
1 pound zucchini, unpeeled, cut into $\frac{1}{2}$-inch slices
1 pound frozen cauliflower florets
about $2\frac{1}{2}$ cups frozen chopped spinach (about 10 ounces)
2 small skinless chicken breasts (about 12 ounces), cut into 1-inch strips
2 tablespoons chopped fresh parsley

1. Spray a large sauce pan with the olive oil and sauté the onion, until soft and translucent, but not brown.
2. Add the garlic slices and stir-fry spices and sauté for another 2 minutes.
3. Add the tomatoes, the vegetable broth, the tomato paste, the chili sauce and salt and pepper to taste. Bring slowly to a boil.
4. Add the zucchini and cook slowly, covered, until almost done, but still crunchy.
5. Meanwhile defrost the cauliflower florets, following the instructions on the packet.

Main Dishes – Poultry, Game and Meat

6. Defrost the spinach, following the instructions on the packet.

7. Add the cauliflower florets and the spinach to the saucepan. Adjust the seasoning. Bring to a boil.

8. Reduce heat and add the chicken strips to the pot, pressing them gently into the mixture with the back of a spoon.

9. Simmer all together for about 10 minutes. Check the chicken for doneness.

10. Serve in big individual plates. Prior to serving, sprinkle with the parsley.

Chili Con Carne
Yield: 4 - 6 servings

Chili con carne is usually made with beef, but here we substitute chicken. Alternatively you can use any other conforming meat, such as turkey, venison, and so on. Also in our recipe here, we substitute beans by eggplant.

The chili is much tastier a day or two after it's cooked, as the flavors develop and the texture becomes richer.

olive oil spray
2 small-medium onion (about 8 ounces), thinly sliced
2 large cloves garlic, crushed
1 carrot, sliced
2 medium celery stalks (about 4 ounces), sliced
2-3 teaspoons dried chili flakes, to taste
1 teaspoon ground cumin
1 teaspoon ground coriander
1 stick cinnamon
3 tablespoons tomato paste
1 good shake of Worcestershire sauce
2-3 medium eggplants (around 20 ounces), unpeeled and cut into bite-size pieces
14-ounce can chopped tomatoes
1 cup red wine
salt to taste
freshly ground black pepper, to taste
2 chicken breasts (around $1\frac{1}{4}$ pound), skinless and fatless, minced
optional: 3 tablespoons fresh coriander leaves, chopped

1. Spray a large saucepan with the olive oil and sauté the onion until soft and translucent, but not brown.
2. Mix in the garlic, carrot and celery and sauté all together for another 2 minutes.

Main Dishes – Poultry, Game and Meat

3. Add the chili flakes, cumin, coriander, cinnamon and coat the veggies with the spices. Mix in the tomato paste and Worcestershire sauce. Heat through for 2 minutes.

4. Add the eggplant and sauté uncovered for about 5 minutes.

5. Add the tomatoes with their juice and the red wine.

6. Season with salt (sparingly) and pepper to taste.

7. Bring to a boil and simmer covered for around 20 minutes, or until the eggplant is done.

8. Sauté the minced chicken separately in an oiled frying pan, taking care to separate it (using a fork to shred) during the cooking process.

9. Blend the meat into the eggplant mixture. If necessary, adjust the seasoning.

10. Optional: add the fresh coriander and simmer all together for 2 minutes.

Conny's Moussaka
Yield: 6 servings

This typical Greek dish is usually made with lamb. All we need to do is substitute the meat with a better fatty acid profile meat, such as chicken (or you can use any other fowl or wild game).
Cheese is not normally part of the traditional Mediterranean dish, but is has become common in Western cooking. The purist will leave it out.

3 pounds eggplant, sliced lengthways into $\frac{1}{4}$-inch thick slices
2 tablespoons olive oil
$1\frac{1}{4}$ pounds chicken breast, skinless and fatless, minced
salt to taste
freshly ground black pepper, to taste
2 jars marinara sauce (14 ounces each) - see footnote[1]
Tabasco sauce, to taste
olive oil spray
optional: $\frac{1}{2}$ cup grated Parmesan (or Mozzarella) cheese (about 2 ounces) – the purist will leave it out

1. Steam the eggplant slices in a steamer for 10 minutes or until cooked. Separate them into three lots. Set aside.
2. Heat the oil in a big nonstick frying pan and sauté the minced chicken, taking care to separate it (using a fork to shred) during the cooking process. The chicken meat should be golden brown.
3. Salt and pepper to taste. Add the marinara sauce to the chicken and heat through all together. Season with the Tabasco.
4. Spray a large-size (and preferably square), table-ready baking dish with olive oil. Cover the bottom with the first lot

---

[1] Any tomato, onion, garlic and herb sauce often sold as a pasta sauce.

Main Dishes – Poultry, Game and Meat

of the eggplant slices. Salt and pepper to taste. Take half of
the chicken and marinara mixture and spread it over the
first eggplant layer.

5. Place the second lot of eggplant in the next layer. Salt and
pepper to taste. Spread the remaining chicken and marinara
mixture over the eggplant slices.

6. Place the third lot of eggplant slices in a final layer to
cover the whole dish. Salt and pepper to taste.

7. Sprinkle with Parmesan or Mozzarella cheese (optional: the
purist will leave it out).

8. Put the dish in the oven at 360°F (180°C) and heat through
for around 10 minutes, or until the cheese is melted.

Main Dishes – Poultry, Game and Meat

Curry Stir-fry Chicken Breast
Yield: 4 servings

A good, conforming, self-contained meal with protein and plant food in good balance. The mild curry spice should just be enough to make the dish piquant. (Hot, pungent curries are to be avoided).

1 tablespoon olive oil
2-3 skinless chicken breasts (about 21 oz), cut into cubes
salt (modest)
freshly ground black pepper, to taste
2 tablespoons cumin seeds
2 medium brown onions (about 12 ounces), thinly sliced
4 medium gloves garlic, crushed
3-4 tablespoons mild curry paste, to taste
2 medium green peppers (about 14 ounces), deseeded and sliced
2 medium red peppers (about 14 ounces), deseeded and sliced
2 cans, 14-ounce each, chopped tomatoes

1. Heat the oil in a large pan or wok. Add the chicken and sauté for a few minutes until golden brown on both sides. Salt and pepper to taste. Set aside on a hot plate and cover.
2. Add the cumin seeds to the pan and stir-fry for 2 minutes. Add the onion and sauté, until soft and translucent, but not brown. Stir in the garlic, add the curry paste and stir well to coat the onion.
3. Add the green peppers and sauté until they soften (green peppers take longer to cook than red ones).
4. Mix in the red peppers and stir-fry for another few minutes.
5. Add the chopped tomatoes. Salt and pepper to taste sparingly. Cover and bring slowly to a boil. Reduce heat and cook for about 10 minutes.
6. Add the chicken cubes, pressing them gently into the mixture with the back of a spoon.
7. Simmer together for about 5 minutes. Check for doneness.

Main Dishes – Poultry, Game and Meat

Hunter's Stew
Yield: 8 servings

This recipe is a classic way of preparing hunted meats. It uses the technique (marinating) of soaking the meat in a flavorful liquid to tenderize the meat and enrich its flavor. In this recipe we use goat but you can try this recipe on other game meat too, e.g. venison, buffalo (bison), wild boar, elk etc.

Marinade:
$\frac{1}{2}$ bottle cheap dry red wine
1 medium onion (about 4 ounces), sliced
3 medium garlic cloves, sliced
1 teaspoon peppercorns
1 tablespoon cinnamon bark pieces
3 bay leaves
3 sprigs fresh oregano or thyme
(or 1 tablespoon dried)

Stew:
2 pounds stewing goat, cut into cubes
2 tablespoons olive oil
3-4 medium white onions (about 1 pound), sliced
5 large gloves garlic, crushed
2 tablespoons tomato paste
4 medium-size green peppers (about 1 pound), deseeded and sliced
5 medium-size zucchini (about 2 pounds), sliced
$\frac{1}{2}$ white cabbage (about 1 pound), sliced
salt to taste
freshly ground black pepper, to taste
2 teaspoons dried Italian seasoning
4 pinches ground coriander
4 pinches ground cumin
Tabasco sauce to taste

Main Dishes – Poultry, Game and Meat

1. Prepare the marinade in a medium-size dish and leave the meat to marinate, covered with a lid or foil, for up to 4 days in the fridge (the meat should be covered by the marinade – if not, turn the meat from time to time).
2. Drain the marinade in a colander and just keep the goat meat, the onion and garlic.
3. In a large frying pan or wok heat half of the oil. Add the goat meat and sauté for a few minutes until golden brown on both sides. Set aside on a plate and cover.
4. Add the rest of the oil to the pan and sauté the onion until it is soft and translucent, but not brown.
5. Add the garlic and sauté for 2 minutes.
6. Mix in the tomato paste, stir well to coat the onion.
7. Add the marinated onion + garlic, the green peppers and sauté for 5 minutes.
8. Mix in the zucchini and cabbage.
9. Season with salt and pepper to taste. Add the Italian seasoning, the coriander, the cumin and the Tabasco sauce to taste.
10. Cook covered until the veggies are almost cooked.
11. Add the goat meat. Simmer all together for 15 minutes.

Sautéed Duck Breast Poached in Red Wine
Yield: 4 servings

Duck breast, without the skin and fat, is very close to the kind of fowl, eaten by our Pleistocene ancestors. Because of its low fat content, expect it to be drier and more chewy than farm bred poultry. One good idea is to serve a cauliflower purée (see recipe page 55) as a side dish.

olive oil spray
2 tablespoons shallot, finely chopped
1 cup red wine
1 bay leaf
1 cup non-fat chicken broth, canned
2 medium cloves garlic, crushed
salt to taste
freshly ground black pepper, to taste
2 duck breasts, skin and fat removed, about 5 - 6 ounces each (without skin)

1. Spray a medium-size frying pan with the olive oil and sauté the shallots on medium heat, until soft and translucent, but not brown. Add the wine and the bay leaf. Bring to a boil. Reduce heat and simmer uncovered for about 8-10 minutes, until the liquid has reduced to about $\frac{1}{2}$ cup.
2. Strain through a sieve. Pour the sauce into a medium-size saucepan. Add the chicken broth and the garlic. Bring to a boil. Season with salt and pepper to taste. Cover and set aside.
3. Sauté the duck breasts in a hot medium-size frying pan (no oil added) on medium-high heat for about 2 minutes on each side. Salt and pepper to taste.
4. Place the duck breasts into the hot broth in the saucepan. Cover and remove from stove. Allow the meat to soak for approximately 10 minutes (the duck meat should still be a little pink inside).

Main Dishes – Poultry, Game and Meat

5. Prior to serving remove the duck breast from the broth and cut in thick slices.

6. You could either divide the duck meat onto 4 individual plates, topped with a little sauce, or you could serve it sliced on a serving plate, topped with a little sauce. The rest of the sauce should be served separately in a sauce boat, so that diners can help themselves to more.

Venison Meatballs
Yield: 4 servings

This makes a hearty and tasty burger style meat dish. The venison is a safe meat that, like all high protein foods, should nevertheless be eaten in restricted quantities.

olive oil spray
2 tablespoons minced shallots
2 medium cloves garlic, crushed
1¼ pound ground venison burger meat
2 eggs
1 teaspoon paprika powder
1 teaspoon Worcester sauce
1 tablespoon chopped fresh parsley (or dried parsley flakes)
½ teaspoon salt
freshly ground black pepper, to taste

1. Spray a small frying pan with olive oil and sauté the shallot rapidly on medium heat until soft and translucent, but not brown.
2. Mix in the garlic and heat again briefly.
3. Place the burger meat in a large bowl.
4. Beat the eggs with a fork in a small bowl together with the remaining ingredients.
5. Add the eggs to the meat and coat the meat equally (the best way is to use your hands).
6. Form patties with your hands, any size you wish to give them.
7. Spray a large frying pan with the oil and sauté the meatballs from both sides until brown. Then cover and cook until the center of the venison burgers is cooked.

Main Dishes – Poultry, Game and Meat

Venison Steak
Yield: 4 servings

We suggest serving the venison steaks and sauce together with a cauliflower purée (see recipe page 55). It makes a fine centerpiece for a festive dinner.

Marinade:
red wine (enough to cover the venison)
1 small red onion, sliced
2 large cloves garlic, crushed
$\frac{1}{2}$ teaspoon grated ginger
1 bay leaf
1 teaspoon grated orange peel

Staples:
about 1 pound wild venison steak, fresh or frozen
2 tablespoons orange juice
olive oil spray
salt to taste
freshly ground black pepper, to taste

1. Prepare the marinade in a medium-size dish and, and whether the venison is fresh or frozen, marinate for 24 hours (covered with a lid or foil). There should be enough marinade to cover the meat (if not, turn the meat from time to time).
2. The following day, remove the steaks and set aside. Strain the marinade through a fine sieve and pour the sauce into a small saucepan. Add the orange juice and bring to a boil. Reduce to half of the original volume. Set aside.
3. Dry the steaks with kitchen paper. Spray both sides of the meat with olive oil and salt and pepper to taste.
4. Spray a non-stick frying pan with the oil and sauté the steaks on medium-high heat for about 2 minutes on each side.
5. Add a little amount of the sauce to the steaks. Cover and simmer on low heat for about 5 minutes, or until the meat is cooked, but still slightly pink inside.
6. Serve the sauce on the side.

CHAPTER 5
Main Dishes
Seafood

Dijon Ahi Tuna
Yield: 2 servings

This is a fine omega-3 rich meal. The same recipe can be used for other types of fish too, such as shark and salmon.

Sauce:
2-3 shallots (about 2 ounces), finely chopped
2 teaspoons Dijon mustard
2 tablespoons olive oil
1 tablespoon fresh lemon juice
$\frac{1}{4}$ teaspoon salt
freshly ground black pepper, to taste
Fish:
2 Ahi Tuna steaks (about 4-5 ounces each)
olive oil spray

1. Combine in a small bowl all the ingredients for the sauce and blend with a hand whisk to obtain a creamy sauce.
2. Coat the tuna steaks on both sides with the mixture.
3. Spray a medium-size baking dish with the olive oil and lay out the fish on the bottom.
4. Pour the rest of the sauce over the fish.
5. Grill for about 5 minutes. Check the fish for doneness.

Crabe St. Jacques au Gratin
Yield: 4 servings

Eat as a starter, or as a main dish accompaniment. The "St. Jacques" style normally employs "bad" ingredients, such as double cream, butter and flour. Here, in this recipe, we achieve a dish with all the same flavor and delicious taste, but without the bad ingredients.

2 cans crab meat (6 ounces net weight each)
2/3 cup clam juice (more or less as needed)
1 pound cauliflower purée - see recipe page 55
2 pinches nutmeg
salt taste
freshly ground black pepper, to taste
olive oil spray
optional: $\frac{1}{2}$ cup grated Swiss cheese (about 2 ounces) - the purist will leave it out

1. Drain the crabmeat thoroughly and capture the liquid in a measuring cup. Set aside the liquid, which will amount to about 2/3 cup. Set aside the crabmeat.
2. In a bowl mix the crab liquid (2/3 cup) with the clam juice (2/3 cup). Blend the cauliflower puree slowly into the liquid with a whisk, until you obtain a smooth consistency.
3. Mix in the crabmeat.
4. Season with the nutmeg, salt and pepper to taste.
5. Spray 4 individual small, ovenproof molds with the olive oil and fill with the mixture.
6. Optional: sprinkle the cheese over the top of the dishes (the purist will leave it out).
7. Brown under the grill, until the surface has a golden color (keeping the dish at a certain distance from the grill).
8. Serve directly to the table in the molds.

Main Dishes – Seafood

Emma's Zucchini and Tuna Gratin
Yield: 6 servings

The challenge of making zucchini into a flavorful dish is successfully achieved by the judicious choice of a wide range of spices. Overall, the dish achieves a good balance of plant food and protein.

olive oil spray
2 small-medium red onion (about 8 ounces), thinly sliced
4 large cloves garlic, crushed
$\frac{1}{4}$ teaspoon hot chili sauce
2 pounds zucchini, unpeeled and thinly sliced
3 teaspoons Italian seasoning
salt to taste
freshly ground black pepper to taste
1 teaspoon lemon juice
6 eggs
2 cans tuna flakes (4.5 ounces net weight, each), drained

1. Spray a large frying pan with the oil and sauté the onion, until it is soft and translucent, but not brown.
2. Mix in the garlic, the chili sauce and sauté all together.
3. Add the zucchini, sprinkle with the Italian seasoning and salt and pepper to taste. Sauté for about 30 minutes, or until done (but still crunchy). Mix in the lemon juice.
4. Meanwhile beat the eggs with a hand-whisk. Salt and pepper to taste.
5. Add the tuna flakes and the cooked zucchini (non-drained) to the eggs. Mix all together, leaving a coarse texture.
6. Spray a loaf mold (10-inches long, 5-inches wide, 3-inches high) with the olive oil and fill with the mixture.
7. Bake in a hot oven at 360° F (180° C) for about 40 minutes. Check the eggs for doneness.
8. Serve hot or cold.

Fish Loaf
Yield: 6 servings

A good, conforming, high protein dish, to serve as part of a main meal. Since it is best served cold, it is also much appreciated at party buffets.

olive oil spray
5 medium cloves garlic, crushed
28-ounce can chopped tomatoes
salt to taste
freshly ground black pepper, to taste
1½ pound cod fillets
6 eggs
1 pinch cayenne pepper, or to taste
4 tablespoons chopped fresh basil

1. Spray a large frying pan with the olive oil and sauté the garlic rapidly.
2. Add the tomatoes and salt and pepper to taste. Cook uncovered over medium heat. When most of the liquid has evaporated, reduce the heat. Simmer, uncovered, stirring frequently, until the tomatoes start to stick to the pan (the cooking time for the tomatoes can be around 50 minutes). Set aside.
3. Meanwhile coarsely chop the raw fish fillets, by hand or in a food processor. Set aside.
4. Beat the eggs in a large mixing bowl with an electric hand-mixer. Add the salt, pepper and cayenne to taste.
5. Mix in the tomatoes, the fish and the basil and coat well with the eggs. If necessary, adjust the seasoning.
6. Spray a large round baking mold (9 or 10 inches diameter) with the olive oil and fill with the mixture.
7. Bake in a hot oven at 360° F (180° C) for 50-60 minutes. Check for doneness.
8. This dish can be served directly in the mold, or allow to cool and then de-mold.

Red Snapper Casablanca
Yield: 4 servings

The subtle, spicy tang of Arabia brings an exotic flavor to this perfect preparation of Red Snapper.

olive oil spray
4 red snapper filets (about 1 pound)
salt to taste
freshly ground black pepper, to taste
1 medium white onion (about 4-5 ounces), finely chopped
1 large red bell pepper (about 8 ounces), seeded and finely chopped
2 cloves garlic, crushed
1 pinch red cayenne pepper, or to taste
$\frac{1}{2}$ teaspoon thyme, fresh or dried
2 tablespoons fresh chopped mint
2 tablespoons fresh lemon juice
1 tablespoon white wine

1. Spray a non-stick frying pan with the olive oil and sauté in a hot pan each side of the fish filets for about 2 minutes, or until done and golden brown. Salt and pepper to taste. Set aside on a serving dish.
2. In the same pan sauté the onion, bell pepper and garlic, until tender and soft.
3. Mix in the cayenne pepper, the thyme, 1 tablespoon of the mint, the lemon juice and the white wine.
4. Simmer all together for 2 minutes. Salt and pepper to taste.
5. Layer the mixture over the fish on the serving dish.
6. Sprinkle with the remaining tablespoon of mint.
7. This dish can be served, either hot or cold.

Spicy Asian Fish
Yield: 4 - 6 servings

This lightly spiced dish gets its piquant and typical Asian flavor from ginger and lemon grass. Most kinds of thick white fish can be used. This dish can be eaten on its own or served with a green salad.

1 tablespoon olive oil
1 pound brown onion, sliced
4 large cloves garlic, crushed
2 tablespoons grated fresh ginger
1 tablespoon finely chopped fresh lemon grass
1 teaspoon ground turmeric
2 tablespoons balsamic vinegar
1 tablespoon fish sauce
1 pound tomatoes, seeded and roughly chopped
salt to taste
freshly ground black pepper, to taste
1½ pounds white, boneless fish fillets (catfish, monkfish etc.), cut into 1-inch cubes
2 tablespoons chopped fresh cilantro leaves

1. Heat the olive oil in a large saucepan and sauté the onion, until it is soft and translucent, but not brown.
2. Stir in the garlic, ginger, lemon grass, turmeric, vinegar and fish sauce and bring slowly to a boil. Reduce heat and simmer, uncovered, for 3 minutes.
3. Stir in the tomatoes and bring slowly to a boil. Salt and pepper to taste. Reduce heat and simmer covered for approximately 10 minutes. The tomatoes should still be crunchy.
4. Fold in the fish and cover with the tomato mixture. Reduce heat and simmer, covered, for 5 minutes, or until the fish is tender and done.
5. Serve sprinkled with the cilantro leaves.

Swordfish on Fennel Bed
Yield: 4 servings

A simply prepared dish. The fennel flavors agreeably complement the chunky swordfish taste. The ratio of vegetables to protein is good at about 3:1 - so it makes a meal in itself.

olive oil spray
2 fennel bulbs (about 20 ounces), thinly sliced
5 tablespoons freshly squeezed orange juice
4-ounce can chopped black olives
$1\frac{1}{4}$ pound Roma tomatoes, seeded and coarsely chopped
salt to taste
freshly ground black pepper, to taste
1 tablespoon olive oil
2 large cloves garlic, crushed
1 pound swordfish steak

1. Trim the green fronds from the fennel bulb and save for garnish. Clean the fennel bulbs, remove the stringy parts (as with celery). Cut each bulb in quarters and slice thinly.
2. Spray a large baking dish with the olive oil spray.
3. Combine fennel, orange juice and olives in a mixing bowl. Spoon the mixture into the baking dish. Lay out the tomatoes over the top. Salt and pepper to taste.
4. Cover with an aluminum foil and bake at 360°F (180°C) for about 30 minutes, stirring once.
5. Meanwhile combine, in a small bowl, the oil, garlic, pepper and salt (to taste) and brush evenly over the fish.
6. Place the fish on top of the cooked vegetables in the baking dish, cover with the foil and bake for another approximately 15 minutes, until the fish is done.

Trout Marrakech
Yield: 2 servings

This is a good conforming fish dish in the Moroccan style.

Fish:
1 trout (about 1 pound), cleaned
salt to taste
freshly ground black pepper, to taste
olive oil spray
1 medium red onion (about 5 ounces), thinly sliced
4 tablespoons white wine
2 pinch saffron (optional)
Stuffing:
2 tablespoons olive oil
1 tablespoon water
1 tablespoon fructose
1 teaspoon cinnamon
2 teaspoons orange blossom water (optional)
salt (moderate)
freshly ground black pepper, to taste
½ cup almond flakes (about 2 ounces)

1. Season the trout on the inside with salt and pepper (moderate). Set aside.
2. Spray a large baking dish with the olive oil and lay out the onion on the bottom of the dish.
3. In a small mixing bowl mix the white wine with the saffron and pour equally over the onion.
4. Stuffing: in a small mixing bowl blend all the ingredients (except the almonds) with a hand-whisk. Stir in the almonds.
5. Fill half of the stuffing inside the trout and place the trout on top of the onion in the baking dish. Spread the remaining stuffing over the top of the fish.
6. Bake in a hot oven at 380°F (190°C) for approximately 30 minutes. Check the fish for doneness.

Tuna and Tomato Bake
Yield: 2 servings

The tuna steak is buried in a deep pile of flavorful tomatoes and onion. It has a good ratio of protein to plant food – about 1 to 4 – and what ingredients! It is laden with healthful fish oils and wondrous micronutrients.

2 pounds fresh tomatoes (or two 14-ounce cans chopped tomatoes)
1 tuna steak (about 10 ounces)
4 large cloves garlic, crushed
1 teaspoon paprika powder
2 teaspoons dried Italian seasoning
salt to taste
freshly ground black pepper, to taste
olive oil spray
2 medium white onions (about 8 ounces), sliced
Tabasco Sauce to taste
1 tablespoon chopped fresh basil

1. Place the tomatoes in a large bowl and pour boiling water over them. Set aside for 1 minute. Drain the tomatoes, peel off the skin and cut into $\frac{1}{2}$-inch thick slices. Set aside in a colander (if you use canned tomatoes, first drain the liquid).
2. Coat the tuna on both sides with 2 crushed garlic cloves, the paprika and 1 teaspoon of the Italian seasoning. Dust lightly with salt and pepper. Set aside. For best taste, prepare the tuna in advance and marinate in the fridge overnight.
3. Spray a medium-size baking dish with the oil and spread out the onion. Coat the onion with another spray of olive oil.
4. Place the tomatoes on top. Distribute the remaining garlic equally into the tomatoes. Salt and pepper to taste. Season with the remaining Italian herbs and Tabasco sauce.

Main Dishes – Seafood

5. Bake in a preheated oven at 360°F (180°C) for 20 minutes.

6. Dig a hole in the cooked mixture and place the tuna in the middle of the vegetables. Cover with the mixture and bake again all together for about 15 minutes, or until the fish is cooked.

7. Prior to serving sprinkle with the chopped basil.

Wahoo Steak and Vegetables
Yield: 2 servings

Wahoo is related to tuna and swordfish which can be used instead. This is a quick and healthy dish. Try serving with more vegetables, such as swiftly blanched green beans.

1 Wahoo steak (about 10 ounces), frozen or fresh
1 tablespoon fresh lemon juice
olive oil spray
1½ cup sliced mushrooms (about 3 ounces)
4 green onions, sliced
1 tablespoon white wine
2 teaspoons Italian herbs, to taste
salt to taste
freshly ground black pepper, to taste
½ teaspoon curry powder
2 medium zucchini (about 12 ounces), sliced
optional: 2 medium-small tomatoes (about 8 ounces), seeded and sliced

1. Rinse the steak and pat it dry (no need to defrost). Sprinkle both sides with the lemon juice and set aside to marinate.
2. Spray a microwave baking dish with the olive oil and layer in the mushrooms and green onion.
3. Over the vegetables, drizzle the white wine and sprinkle half of the Italian herbs. Salt and pepper to taste.
4. Sprinkle both sides of the Wahoo steak with curry powder and spray with olive oil. Place the fish on top of the mushroom and onion mixture.
5. Lay out the zucchini slices over the steak and season with the remaining Italian herbs. Salt and pepper to taste. Spray a little olive oil over the top. Optional: place the tomatoes on top of the zucchini and adjust the seasoning.
6. Cover and cook in the microwave on 600 watts for about 10 minutes. Check the fish and vegetables for doneness.

CHAPTER 6
Desserts

Apricot Tart
Yield: 8 servings

Try the recipe with other fruits. For example peaches or nectarines.

21 ounces (about) fresh apricots
Dough:
2 eggs
2 teaspoons fructose
2 teaspoons vanilla extract
2 teaspoons ground cinnamon
3 tablespoons olive oil
1¼ cup (about 4½ ounces) almond meal (depending on egg size)
Dressing:
olive oil spray
1 tablespoon fructose
optional: 2 teaspoons almond meal

1. Wash and dry the apricots. Cut them in halves. Set aside.
2. To prepare the dough, beat the eggs with an electric hand-mixer in a medium-size mixing bowl. Add all the dough ingredients and blend to obtain a smooth pastry.
3. Spray a round tart mold (10-inches diameter) with the olive oil and cover the bottom by spreading the dough in a thin layer, leaving a low rim around the edge. Prick the bottom of the dough with a fork.
4. Bake in a preheated oven at 360°F (180°C) for 5 minutes only, to get the mixture to set. Allow to cool.
5. Layer the apricots cut-side up, in concentric circles, on top of the dough.

Desserts

6. Sprinkle the apricots with the fructose and the 2 teaspoons of almond meal (optional), in order to soak up the fruit juice during the cooking.

7. Return the tart to the oven at 360°F (180°C) for about 30 minutes, or until the dough is golden brown. When you take it out of the oven, there might be a film of liquid left on the surface, which will glaze when cooling off.

Banana Pancake
Yield: up to 8 servings

This makes a sweet pancake-style dessert. The use of ripe banana and raisins does mean that it has quite a high sugar content (there is no need for additional fructose). For this reason, just treat the dish as a sweetmeat and eat sparingly.

4 tablespoons raisins (about 2 ounces)
1 tablespoon dark rum
1 banana, ripe
1 teaspoon lemon juice
3 eggs
1 teaspoon ground cinnamon
1 teaspoon vanilla extract
1 tablespoon olive oil
2 tablespoons almond meal
2 tablespoons chopped nuts
olive oil spray

1. In a small bowl soak the raisins in hot water for about 10 minutes. Drain the raisins, add the rum and mix well. Set aside.
2. With a fork mash the banana and mix in the lemon juice. Set aside.
3. In a medium-size bowl beat the eggs with an electric hand-mixer. Mix in the cinnamon, vanilla extract and olive oil. Add the almond meal and beat all together. Blend in the mashed banana and chopped nuts.
4. Spray a round and flat baking dish (10-12 inches diameter) with the olive oil and spread the mixture in a thin layer, so it looks like a pancake.
5. Spread out the raisins evenly over the surface of the dish and press in with a fork.
6. Bake in a preheated oven at 340°F (170°C) for about 15 minutes, or until the center of the pancake is cooked.

Chocolate Brownie
Yield: about 6 servings

Remarkably, this confection steers its way through a variety of potential pitfalls to provide a brownie that is quite delicious and harmless. Because the dish is energy dense, it should be eaten in controlled quantities

2 bars (3½ oz each) dark chocolate, min. 70% cocoa solids
¾ cup almond milk
1 tablespoon dark rum
4 eggs
1 tablespoon fructose, or to taste
1 teaspoon vanilla extract
(optional for Christmas: ½ teaspoon allspice)
2 tablespoons almond meal
1 tablespoon flaked almonds

1. Break the chocolate into small pieces and put into a medium-size microwave-proof bowl. Add the almond milk and rum.
2. Melt the mixture at half power (about 300 watts) in a microwave oven for approximately 3 minutes. Check and stir twice. The chocolate should be melted, but avoid overheating.
3. In a medium-size mixing bowl beat the eggs with an electric hand-mixer. Blend in the fructose, vanilla extract, allspice (optional for Christmas) and almond meal.
4. Add the egg mixture to the chocolate mixture and blend to a smooth consistency.
5. Spoon the mixture into an oiled muffin sheet. Sprinkle the almond flakes over the surface.
6. Bake in a preheated oven at 360°F (180°C) for about 15 minutes. Check for doneness.
7. De-mold the brownies, but do not stack them.

Chocolate Cookies
Yield: up to 20 cookies (depending on size)

This makes a delicious, chocolate covered cookie with a moist consistency. It is a conforming sweetmeat of the high protein type and should be consumed in limited quantities. Try to eat no more than two at a sitting! Good to eat as a light dessert or with a cup of tea or coffee.
To give a typical Christmas flavor you can add allspice to the chocolate coating.

4 egg whites
1 pinch salt
2 tablespoons fructose
optional for Christmas: 1 tablespoon allspice, or to taste
$2\frac{1}{4}$ cups almond meal (or hazelnut meal) – increase the quantity by up to $\frac{1}{4}$ cup to achieve a dough-like consistency
optional: $\frac{1}{2}$ cup chopped almonds (about $2\frac{1}{2}$ ounces)
olive oil spray
Coating:
$\frac{1}{2}$ bar (of a $3\frac{1}{2}$ oz bar) dark chocolate, min. 70% cocoa solids
1 teaspoon orange extract
1 tablespoon rum, dark and flavorful
3 tablespoons fresh orange juice
Garnish:
$1\frac{1}{2}$ tablespoons unsweetened grated coconut
2 teaspoons fructose
alternatively: 3 tablespoons chopped almond (or hazelnut)

1. Take a medium-size mixing bowl and with an electric hand-mixer beat the egg whites with the pinch of salt to a stiff consistency. Mix in the fructose and (optional for Christmas) the allspice.

Desserts

2. Add the nut meal and blend well to obtain a smooth paste. Add the chopped almonds (optional).

3. Spray a cookie sheet with olive oil. Shape approximately 20 cookies by hand and lay out on the baking sheet.

4. Bake in a hot oven at 360° F (180° C), for 10-12 minutes. Check for doneness. Allow the cookies to cool down.

5. **Coating**: break the chocolate into small pieces and put into a small microwave-proof bowl. Add the orange extract, rum and orange juice and melt the mixture in the microwave oven at half power (about 300 watts) for approximately $1\frac{1}{2}$ minutes, stirring once halfway through, until the chocolate is melted.

6. Coat the upper-half of the cookies with the chocolate mixture.

7. **Garnish**: mix the coconut powder with the fructose in a little bowl and sprinkle over the chocolate cookies.

(Alternatively, instead of the coconut garnish: sprinkle each chocolate covered cookie with approximately $\frac{1}{2}$ teaspoon of chopped almonds - or hazelnuts - and press them into the chocolate with a spatula).

8. Allow the cookies to cool (the chocolate coating has to be solid again). They are now ready for consumption. Keep them in a box in your fridge, if you want to store them for more than 2-3 days.

Chocolate Delight
Yield: 8 servings

Remarkably, this confection steers its way through a variety of potential pitfalls to provide a chocolate gateau that is quite delicious. Because the dish is fundamentally energy dense, you should limit yourself to just one serving at a sitting.

2 bars ($3\frac{1}{2}$ oz each) dark chocolate, min. 70% cocoa solids
$\frac{3}{4}$ cup almond milk
1 tablespoon dark rum
4 eggs
2 tablespoons olive oil
1 teaspoon orange extract
3 tablespoons diabetic orange marmalade
3 tablespoons almond meal
olive oil spray

1. Break the chocolate into small pieces and put into a medium-size microwave-proof bowl. Add the almond milk and rum.
2. Melt the mixture at half power (about 300 watts) in a microwave oven for approximately 3 minutes. Check and stir twice. The chocolate should be melted, but avoid overheating.
3. In a medium-size mixing bowl beat the eggs with an electric hand-mixer. Blend in the olive oil, orange extract, orange marmalade and almond meal.
4. Add the chocolate mixture to the eggs and blend to a smooth consistency.
5. Spray a round and flat, table-ready baking dish (10-inches diameter) with the olive oil. Slowly pour the mixture into it.
6. Bake in a preheated oven at 340°F (170°C) for about 15 minutes. The center of this chocolate delight should still be slightly moist. Allow to cool.

Chocolate Mousse
Yield: 4 servings

This dish is an interesting example of how a superb dessert can be made from high density chocolate and fructose.

2 bars (3½ oz each) dark chocolate, 70% min. cocoa solids
2 teaspoons orange extract
4 tablespoons flavorful rum
2 teaspoons instant coffee
4 tablespoons water
4 eggs, organic free-range
1 tablespoon fructose
2 teaspoons grated orange peel

1. Break the chocolate into small pieces and put into a medium-size microwave-proof bowl. Add the orange extract, the rum, the instant coffee and the water.
2. Melt the mixture at half power (about 300 watts) in a microwave oven for approximately 3 minutes. Check and stir twice. The chocolate should be melted, but avoid overheating. Set aside.
3. Take 2 medium-size mixing bowls, carefully break the eggs and separate the yolks from the whites.
4. In the first bowl, mix the egg yolks and the fructose to a creamy texture with an electric hand-mixer. Add 1 teaspoon grated orange peel to the mixture. Set aside.
5. In the second bowl, beat the egg whites with an electric hand-mixer, until very stiff (you can also choose to do it in your food processor).
6. Add the yolk/sugar mixture slowly to the cooled down, but still warm, chocolate mixture. Blend to a smooth consistency.
7. Add the egg whites progressively to the mixture, stirring carefully to obtain a smooth consistency.
8. Spoon the mixture into 4 individual dessert cups and sprinkle the remaining orange peel over the top.
9. Conserve in a refrigerator for a minimum of 5 hours (ideally make the mousse the day before consumption).

Chocolate Petits Fours
Yield: about 20

This makes the delicious French style bite-sized sweets eaten at the end of the meal.

Equipment: 25-30 small fluted paper cups (about $1\frac{1}{4}$ -inch diameter)

20 – 25 raisins
3 tablespoons + 1 teaspoon dark rum
1 orange, preferably organic
1 bar ($3\frac{1}{2}$ oz) dark chocolate, 70% minimum cocoa solids
2 teaspoons orange extract
Garnish:
1 tablespoon unsweetened grated coconut
1 teaspoon fructose

1. In a small bowl soak the raisins in hot water for about 10 minutes. Drain the raisins, add 1 teaspoon of rum and mix well. Set aside.
2. Grate the orange skin and set aside the gratings. Squeeze the orange and set aside the juice.
3. Break the chocolate into small pieces and put into a small microwave-proof bowl. Add the remaining 3 tablespoons of rum, 4 tablespoons of the orange juice and the orange extract. Melt the mixture at half power (about 300 watts) in a microwave oven for approximately 2 minutes. Check and stir twice. The chocolate should be melted, but avoid overheating.
4. Add the orange gratings.
5. Spoon the chocolate mixture into the fluted paper cups.
6. With a teaspoon press 1 raisin into the center of each cup.
7. In a small cup, mix the grated coconut with the fructose and sprinkle over the top of the petit fours.
8. Allow to cool to the point where the chocolate sets.

Coconut Muffins
Yield: 10-12 muffins

These muffins are delicious for continental breakfast, at tea-time or as an occasional snack.

4 tablespoons raisins (about 2 ounces)
2 tablespoons dark rum
3 eggs
$\frac{3}{4}$ cups almond milk
6 tablespoons ($\frac{1}{2}$ cup) almond meal
2 teaspoons vanilla extract
1 teaspoon lemon juice
1 tablespoon olive oil
1 cup unsweetened grated coconut ($3\frac{1}{2}$ ounces)
3 tablespoons diabetic orange marmalade
1 teaspoon fructose, or to taste
olive oil spray
2 squares (maximum a quarter of a $3\frac{1}{2}$ oz bar) dark chocolate (minimum 70% cocoa solids), broken into small chips

1. In a small bowl soak the raisins in hot water for about 10 minutes. Drain, add the rum and mix well. Set aside.
2. In a medium-size mixing bowl beat the eggs with an electric hand-mixer. Mix in the almond milk, the almond meal, the vanilla extract, the lemon juice, the olive oil and the coconut. Blend to a smooth consistency.
3. Blend in the orange marmalade and sweeten with fructose to taste, bearing in mind that you will add other sweetening ingredients (the raisins and the chocolate).
4. Spray 10 fluted muffin molds ($2\frac{1}{2}$-inches diameter) with the olive oil and fill with the mixture.
5. With a fork press raisins and chocolate chips into each muffin, distributing them equally.
6. Bake in a preheated oven at 360°F (180°C) for 30-40 minutes, or until the center of the muffins is cooked and they have a golden brown color.

Coconut Pancake
Yield: Up to 8 servings

This makes an aromatic and flavorful, sweetish yet safe, dessert. It is quite rich and so just eat by the slice.

4 tablespoons raisins (about 2 ounces)
1 tablespoon dark rum
1 banana, ripe
1 teaspoon lemon juice
3 eggs
1 teaspoon vanilla extract
1 tablespoon olive oil
1/3 cup (or 5 tablespoons) almond milk
2 tablespoons almond meal
5 tablespoons unsweetened grated coconut
fructose to taste
olive oil spray

1. In a small bowl soak the raisins in hot water for about 10 minutes. Drain, add the rum and mix well. Set aside.
2. With a fork mash the banana and mix in the lemon juice. Set aside.
3. In a medium-size mixing bowl beat the eggs with an electric hand-mixer. Mix in the vanilla extract and olive oil. Add the almond milk, the almond meal and coconut. Add the mashed banana and sweeten with fructose to taste, bearing in mind that you will add other sweetening ingredients (the raisins).
4. Spray a round and flat baking dish (approximately 10-12 inches diameter) with the olive oil and spread the mixture in a thin layer, so it looks like a pancake.
5. Spread out the raisins evenly over the surface of the dish and press in with a fork.
6. Bake in a preheated oven at 340°F (170°C) for about 15 minutes, or until the center of the pancake is cooked.

Devilled Strawberries
Yield: 4 servings

This is a fresh, tingling way to spice up strawberries. Strawberries (together with raspberries) are one of the few fruits that are fine eaten at the end of a meal.

1 pound fresh strawberries
2 teaspoons fructose
freshly ground black pepper, to taste
1 tablespoon raspberry vinegar
Garnish:
about 30 fresh mint leaves

1. Wash and dry the strawberries. Remove stalks. Cut any big strawberries in half.
2. Place all the strawberries in a medium-size bowl. Sprinkle with the fructose sparingly, and the pepper generously (or to taste). Pour the vinegar equally over the berries. Toss carefully.
3. Best made prior to serving, but allow to chill for 10 minutes.
4. Serve on individual dessert plates and garnish each plate with a few scattered mint leaves.

Jeanne's Chocolate Marble Cake
Yield: 12 servings (slices)

This makes a delicious, fully conforming marble cake that will delight children and adults alike.

5 eggs
4 tablespoons fructose, or to taste
4 tablespoons olive oil
2 cups almond meal (7 ounces)
2 teaspoons vanilla extract
$\frac{1}{2}$ cup cocoa powder (about 2 ounces)
1 tablespoon dark rum
4 tablespoons almond milk (more - if needed)
olive oil spray

1. In a medium-size mixing bowl beat the eggs with an electric hand-mixer. Blend in 3 tablespoons of fructose and 3 tablespoons of olive oil. Add the almond meal and blend to obtain a smooth paste.
2. Split this dough into two equal portions into 2 separate mixing bowls:
3. In one portion blend in the vanilla extract. This will be the "light colored dough".
4. In the second portion blend in the remaining 1 tablespoon of fructose, the remaining 1 tablespoon of olive oil, the cocoa powder, the rum and the almond milk (add more, if the "dough" is too thick). This will be the "dark colored dough".
5. Spray a cake mold (10-inches long, 5-inches wide, 3-inches high) with the olive oil. Pour light colored and dark colored dough layers randomly into the mold. You can play with the proportions of light and dark layers to make a yet more interesting "marbling".
6. Bake in a pre-heated oven at 340°F (170°C) for about 30 minutes.
7. Check for doneness. The center should be cooked and firm.

Lemon Tart
Yield: up to 12 servings

Here I have succeeded in creating the same tangy lemon curd, nutty pastry and meringue, as in conventional recipes, but using healthy ingredients! This recipe uses fructose as usual (instead of sugar) which is a huge improvement. Nevertheless, the amounts required in this recipe are large, even for fructose, so the purist will eat this dish moderately.

Dough:
1 egg
2 teaspoons fructose
3 tablespoons olive oil
1 cup almond meal (about $3\frac{1}{2}$ ounces)
olive oil spray

Filling:
2 eggs
5 tablespoons fructose, or to taste
2 tablespoons olive oil
$\frac{1}{2}$ cup freshly squeezed lemon juice
zest of 2 large lemons, finely grated

Meringue (optional):
2 egg whites
3 tablespoons fructose

Dough:
1. In a medium-size mixing bowl, beat the egg, fructose and oil with an electric hand-mixer. Add the almond meal and blend all together, to obtain a smooth pastry.
2. Spray a round baking dish ($9\frac{1}{2}$-inches diameter) with the olive oil and, by patting with a small spatula, spread out the dough in a thin layer (just to cover the bottom of the dish), leaving a low rim around the edge. Prick the bottom of the dough with a fork.

Desserts

3. Bake in a preheated oven at 340°F (170°C) for 5 minutes only, to set the dough. Allow to cool.

Filling:

4. In the meantime prepare the lemon filling in a medium-size mixing bowl. Blend the eggs, fructose and oil with an electric hand-mixer. Mix in the lemon juice and lemon gratings.

5. Slowly pour the filling into the baking dish on top of the dough.

6. Lower the oven temperature to 300°F (150°C) and bake for about 30 minutes, or until the filling is cooked. Remove the tart from the oven.

Meringue (optional):

7. Pre-heat the grill.

8. Meanwhile beat in a medium-size mixing bowl the egg whites with an electric hand-mixer to a stiff consistency. Whisk the fructose carefully into the eggs.

9. with a spatula spread out the meringue mixture over the top of the lemon tart.

10. Grill for about 2 minutes, until the meringue has a golden brown color.

11. Allow the tart to cool completely before serving.

Mock Cheese Flan
Yield: 8 - 10 servings

This makes a delicious, conforming flan that can be eaten at any time of day -- for example, as a quick continental breakfast or at afternoon tea. This is a dense dish that is rich in protein, so ration yourself!

3 tablespoons raisins (about 1.5 ounces)
1 tablespoon dark rum
$1\frac{1}{2}$ cup blanched almonds (8 ounces)
$\frac{1}{2}$ cup water
2 eggs
3 tablespoons fructose, or to taste
3 tablespoons olive oil
$\frac{1}{4}$ teaspoon allspice
2 teaspoons vanilla extract
$\frac{1}{2}$ cup freshly squeezed lemon juice
olive oil spray

1. In a small bowl soak the raisins in hot water for about 10 minutes. Drain, add the rum and mix well. Set aside.
2. Place the almonds in a food processor or blender and grind into flour.
3. Add the remaining ingredients (except the olive oil spray) and blend until you obtain a very creamy texture.
4. Mix in the raisins.
5. Spray a round baking mold (about $9\frac{1}{2}$-inches diameter) with the olive oil. Fill in the mixture. Alternatively you can fill the mixture into individual ramekins.
6. Bake in a hot oven at 340°F (170°C) for about 20 minutes, or until the center of the flan is cooked.
7. Allow the flan to cool down. Serve in the dish.

Nicole's Apple Pie
Yield: up to 12 servings

Try the recipe also with other fruits. For example: apricots, nectarines, apples, plums...
Diabetic jam uses a low glycemic bulk sweetener such as sorbitol. This is fine.

Filling:
4 tablespoons raisins (about 2 ounces)
1 tablespoon dark rum
olive oil spray
2 medium-size apples (about 14 ounces), unpeeled and sliced
2 teaspoons fructose
$2\frac{1}{2}$ tablespoons diabetic orange marmalade

Dough:
5 eggs
2 tablespoons olive oil
5 tablespoons unsweetened grated coconut
2 teaspoons fructose
2 teaspoons ground cinnamon
1 cup almond meal (about $3\frac{1}{2}$ ounces)

1. **Filling:** In a small bowl soak the raisins in hot water for about 10 minutes. Drain, add the rum and mix well. Set aside.
2. Spray a medium size frying pan with the olive oil and sauté the apples, until they are tender, but not mushy. Add the fructose and stir in the raisins.
3. **Dough:** meanwhile beat the eggs with an electric hand-mixer in a medium-size mixing bowl. Add all the dough ingredients and blend to obtain a smooth pastry.

Desserts

4. Spray a round pie dish (10-inches diameter) with the olive oil and spread out a small part of the dough in a thin layer (just to cover the bottom of the dish), leaving a low rim around the edge. Prick the bottom of the dough with a fork.

5. Bake in a preheated oven at 360°F (180°C) for 5 minutes only, to set the dough. Allow to cool.

6. Spread the diabetic marmalade on top of the bottom pie crust.

7. Lay out the apples slices on top of the jam, keeping the edge of the crust free. Spread the remaining dough over the fruits.

8. Return the pie to the oven and bake at 360°F (180°C) for about 20 minutes. Check for doneness.

9. Allow the pie to cool down. De-mold by putting a serving plate on top of the pie and turning the whole lot over. Then lift off the mold, so that the nicely formed underside of the pie is on top.

Orange Cake
Yield: 10-12 servings (slices)

This makes a delicious, conforming cake that can be eaten at any time of day, for example, for a quick continental breakfast or at afternoon tea. This is a dense dish that is rich in protein, so ration yourself to no more than two slices at a time!

1 large orange, preferably organic
1 large lemon, preferably organic
5 eggs
4 tablespoons fructose, or to taste
2 teaspoons ground mixed spices
1 tablespoon olive oil
1 2/3 cup almond meal (about 6 ounces)
4 tablespoons diabetic orange marmalade
olive oil spray

1. Grate the orange and lemon skin and set aside the gratings.
2. Squeeze the orange and lemon to obtain together about 1 cup of juice with its pulp. Set aside.
3. In a medium-size mixing bowl beat the eggs with an electric hand-mixer. Mix in the fructose, mixed spices and olive oil.
4. Blend in the almond meal and the orange and lemon juice with its pulp.
5. Add the orange and lemon gratings and the orange marmalade to the mixture.
6. Spray a loaf mold (10-inches long, 5-inches wide, 3-inches high) with the olive oil and fill with the mixture.
7. Bake in a hot oven at 360°F (180°C) for 30-40 minutes. Check the center for doneness.
8. Allow the cake to cool down. De-mold or serve in the loaf mold.

Raspberry Coulis
Yield: about 1½ cups

This coulis serves as an accompaniment to a wide variety of desserts. It goes particularly well with chocolate desserts. It can be served warm or chilled, depending on the dessert.

1 packet frozen raspberries (12 ounces)
3 tablespoons fructose
1 teaspoon lemon juice

1. Defrost the raspberries in a colander, but collect the juice.
2. Mix the raspberries and juice in a food processor or blender.
3. Rub the puree with a wooden spoon through a sieve, to strain out the seeds. This needs a little time to do.
4. Mix in the fructose and lemon juice.

Raspberry Crumble
Yield: 4 servings

Unlike a conventional fruit crumble, the fruit here is not stewed. The frozen raspberries already have the right consistency. The dish makes a delicious dessert to be eating in moderate quantities. Raspberries, particularly cooked, do not pose a food-combining question.

1 packet frozen raspberries (about 12 ounces)
olive oil spray
1 tablespoon fructose, or to taste
Crumble topping (dough):
2 egg yolks
3 tablespoons olive oil
1 tablespoon fructose
$1\frac{1}{2}$ cups almond meal (5 oz –or more, depending on egg size)

1. Defrost the raspberries and set aside.
2. Spray a medium-size baking dish with the olive oil and spread out the fruits and one tablespoon only of the fruit juice. Sprinkle 1 tablespoon of fructose over the raspberries.
Crumble topping (dough):
3. In a medium-size mixing bowl beat the egg yolks, olive oil and fructose with a hand-whisk. Add the almond meal and by hand, knead the mixture into a ball.
4. Leave the dough ball to rest in the fridge for at least one hour, the time needed for the almond meal to thoroughly absorb the oil (if not, the almond meal will suck up the raspberry juice during the cooking process, making a kind of doughy porridge). It will now be easy to crumble and to cook.
5. By hand, crumble the dough ball over the fruit.
6. Bake in a hot oven at 360° F (180° C) for about 10 minutes. Check for doneness.

Raspberry Sorbet
Yield: 4 servings

A classic sorbet that is safe to eat.

1 packet frozen raspberries (12 ounces)
$\frac{1}{4}$ cup water
3 tablespoons fructose, or to taste
2 egg whites
2 teaspoons freshly squeezed lemon juice

1. Defrost the raspberries in a colander, but collect the juice.
2. Place the berries with their juice, together with the water and fructose, in a small saucepan and bring to a boil. Cook on low heat for about 5 minutes. Allow to cool.
3. Place the egg whites in a blender (or food processor); add the cooled berries and the lemon juice. Puree all together.
4. Place the mixture in an ice cream maker and proceed following the instructions of the machine.

If you don't have an ice cream maker then just place the mixture in a freezer-proof bowl, which you then place in the freezer. In this case you need, from time to time, to fold the frozen edges in towards the middle and so entrain air bubbles to lighten the mixture. Do this after 1 hour, once more after the second hour, and then every 30 minutes for the next 2 hours.

Red Berry Fairy Muffins
Yield: 6 servings

Missing your continental breakfast? Here is a simple solution. These muffins are delicious with a cup of coffee in the morning – or indeed at any time of day.

1 small punnet fresh raspberries or strawberries (about 5½ ounces)
3 tablespoons fructose
1 teaspoon orange extract
2 egg whites
½ cup well packed almond meal (about 2 ounces)
olive oil spray

1. Check the raspberries for cleanliness, wiping as necessary - don't wash. Set aside six raspberries for decoration. If you use strawberries, wash them carefully and wipe dry. Set aside 3 strawberries -cut in half- for decoration. Cut the remaining strawberries into small pieces.
2. Sprinkle the berries with 1 tablespoon of fructose and the orange extract. Set aside.
3. With an electric hand-mixer beat the egg whites in a medium-size mixing bowl to a stiff consistency. Slowly add the remaining fructose, beating all the while. Slowly mix in the almond meal. Fold in the berries.
4. Spray a 6-mold muffin tray with the olive oil. Divide the mixture equally into each mold.
5. Cook in a preheated oven at 350° F (175° C) for about 20 minutes, or until golden brown.
6. Check for doneness. Remove the tray from the oven and set aside to cool.
7. De-mold the Fairy Muffins. Decorate each muffin with one raspberry, or 1 strawberry half, and serve either warm or cold.

Rich Christmas Cake
Yield: 12 - 14 servings (slices)

Yes, your Christmas can still have its cake – and you can eat it too!

This recipe contains all the special Christmassy ingredients, but avoids the pitfalls of bad fats, starches and sugars. Your guests won't know the difference.

1 medium orange, preferably organic
5 tablespoons raisins (2 ounces)
½ cup chopped dried figs (about 5 figs)
3 tablespoons rum, dark and flavorful
5 eggs
2 tablespoons olive oil
2 teaspoons vanilla extract
2 teaspoons orange extract
½ cup almond milk
2 1/3 cups almond meal (about 8.5 ounces) – more if needed for the thickness of the cake
5 tablespoons diabetic orange marmalade
2 cups mixed raw nuts (chopped almonds, walnuts and pecan nuts in pieces - about 9 ounces)
½ cup stoned and chopped dates (about 8 small dates)
1 tablespoon allspice (or mixed spices), or more to taste
2 teaspoons fructose, or to taste
olive oil spray

1. Grate the orange skin and set aside the gratings. Squeeze the orange to obtain about ¼ cup of juice. Set aside.
2. In a small bowl soak the raisins in hot water for about 10 minutes. Drain the raisins. Put back in the bowl and add the chopped figs. Add the rum and mix well. Set aside.

Desserts

3. Meanwhile take a medium-size mixing bowl, and with an electric hand-mixer, beat the eggs with the olive oil, the vanilla extract and the orange extract.

4. Mix in the almond milk and orange juice. Fold in the almond meal. Add the orange marmalade, the orange peel gratings, the mixed nuts, dates, raisins and figs with the rum.

5. Add the allspice (or mixed spices) to taste. Add the fructose to taste.

6. Spray a loaf mold (10-inches long, 5-inches wide, 3-inches high) with the olive oil and fill with the mixture. Bake in a hot oven at 360°F (180°C) for 40 – 45 minutes.

7. Check for doneness (the center of the cake should be cooked).

8. Allow the cake to cool down. De-mold (or serve in the loaf mold).

Strawberry Mousse
Yield 4-6 servings

This dessert can also be made with fresh strawberries. But note that frozen fruits tend to have more juice.
Seaweed gel (e.g."Agar Agar") can be found in every Health Food Store.

1 pound strawberries, frozen
2 tablespoons seaweed gel ("Agar Agar")
2 tablespoons (more or less – to taste) fructose
$\frac{1}{2}$ teaspoon lemon
3 egg whites

1. Set aside 3 whole strawberries for decoration. Cut them in half.
2. Defrost the remaining strawberries in a bowl, to keep all of their juice. Purée the strawberries and their juice in a blender.
3. Take 8 tablespoons of the puree and bring slowly to a boil in a small pan. Add the seaweed gel flakes and bring to a boil, following the instructions on the packet.
4. Stir this mixture into the strawberry puree and blend well together.
5. Mix in the fructose (more or less – to taste) and lemon juice.
6. With an electric hand-mixer beat the egg whites in a medium-size mixing bowl to a stiff consistency.
7. Add the egg whites to the strawberry puree.
8. Divide the strawberry mixture equally among 4 or 6 dessert glasses or ramekins. Top each serving with a strawberry half.
9. Cover and refrigerate until set (at least 4 hours), or until the next day.

INDEX

INDEX

INDEX

DESSERTS

AFTERWORD
From Geoff Bond

I passionately believe in the insights contained in the science of nutritional anthropology. My driving motivation is to stimulate everyone, no matter what your origins and background, to improve your lives. I hope that this recipe book has inspired and encouraged you to know more. Your first port of call should be my website: www.TheBondEffect.com. There you will find online support, speaking engagements, breaking news, updates, hints and tips, and much more. In addition, you can acquire access to many other support materials.

Deadly Harvest - The Bond Effect "Bible"
ISBN: 978-0-7570-0142-0

As a nutritional anthropologist, I have combined the latest scientific research with insightful studies of primitive tribal lifestyles to understand how to live in a way our body recognizes. With Deadly Harvest in hand, you will come to see how diseases like cancer, heart disease, stroke, diabetes, obesity, arthritis, osteoporosis, allergies, ADHD, autism and Alzheimer's are not inevitable, but are optional. They are due to the mismatch between the lifestyle designed by our evolutionary history, and the lifestyle we live today. Fully explained in plain English, you will understand how modern diets are truly killing us, and what you can do to improve our health, combat illnesses, and live longer. It provides an easy-to-follow blueprint to take back control of your life.

The Bond Effect Newsletter
Everyone serious about adopting the Bond Effect will find the monthly newsletter an indispensable aid to keep focused on the essentials. The Bond Effect newsletter takes no advertising – and so it is free to give an honest, straight-from-the-shoulder, Bond Effect viewpoint. More at www.TheBondEffect.com.